BEAUTY THROUGH BROKEN WINDOWS

BEAUTY THROUGH BROKEN WINDOWS

Empowering Edmund Rice's Vision Today

Edited by Aidan Donaldson
and Denis Gleeson

VERITAS

Published 2022 by
Veritas Publications
7–8 Lower Abbey Street
Dublin 1
Ireland
publications@veritas.ie
www.veritas.ie

ISBN 978 1 80097 028 1

Copyright © Aidan Donaldson and Denis Gleeson, 2022

10 9 8 7 6 5 4 3 2 1

The material in this publication is protected by copyright law. Except as may be permitted by law, no part of the material may be reproduced (including by storage in a retrieval system) or transmitted in any form or by any means, adapted, rented or lent without the written permission of the copyright owners. Applications for permissions should be addressed to the publisher.

A catalogue record for this book is available from the British Library.

The lines from 'East Coker' by T.S. Eliot are reprinted from *Four Quartets* (1943), published by Faber and Faber Ltd. Used with permission.

Every effort has been made to contact the copyright holders of the material reproduced herein. If any infringement of copyright has occurred, the owners of such copyright are requested to contact the publisher.

Designed and typeset by Padraig McCormack, Veritas Publications
Cover image: istockphoto.com
Printed in the Republic of Ireland by SPRINT-print Ltd, Dublin

Veritas Publications is a member of Publishing Ireland.

Veritas books are printed on paper made from the wood pulp of managed forests. For every tree felled, at least one tree is planted, thereby renewing natural resources.

Contents

FOREWORD: Looking out the Window with Edmund Rice   7
Jim Deeds

ACKNOWLEDGEMENTS   11

INTRODUCTION   13

Making God Visible Where God Seems Invisible   21
Philip Pinto

A World and a Church Spiritually Impoverished   29
Denis Gleeson

A Window on 2020: A Year of Converging Crises   41
Lorna Gold

Working with the Poorest and the Finest:
'We Are What We Are'   53
Pádraig Ó Fainín

Walking Through Walls:
Fr Gerry Reynolds' Witness against a Divided Christianity   63
Gladys Ganiel

A Pilgrimage for Justice and Peace   75
Lesley O'Connor

Terra Nullius, Australian Indigenous Policy
and the Charism of Edmund Rice   89
Darryl Cronin

Refugees and Racism: Now is Not the Time to be Silent   103
Phil Glendenning

Education, Exclusion and Hope   117
Don O'Leary

For I Was Hungry and You Gave Me Food:
Food before Empowerment 129
John McCourt

God Comes to Us in Disguise 141
Peter McVerry

Breaking Down Racial and Ethnic
Barriers to Spiritual Direction 151
Don Bisson

New Paths for the Church and for Integral Ecology:
A Challenge for the Universal Church 161
Sheila Curran

The Spiritual Challenges of Later Life 173
Una Agnew

Love Through Little Windows:
Reflections on the Paradox and Power of Vulnerability 185
Maria Garvey

Lifting the Veil and Restoring Compassion to Our Eyes 195
Aidan Donaldson

Learn to Live Together as Brothers
and Sisters or Perish as Fools 207
Martin Byrne

Faith and a Better World:
Embracing the Mission to Shape the World of Tomorrow 219
Michel Camdessus

POSTSCRIPT: Looking out the Window
onto the World and Responding as God Asks 233
Angela Miyanda

CONTRIBUTORS 237

Foreword
LOOKING OUT THE WINDOW WITH EDMUND RICE

Jim Deeds

1983. Belfast. I sat in a classroom wearing an ill-fitting uniform (bought big so that I could get good use out of it) and sporting the wide eyes of a first-year pupil who had gone from being a big fish in the wee pond of the primary school to a wee fish in the oh-so-big pond of St Mary's Christian Brothers' Grammar School on the Glen Road. I looked about me at the other boys, most wearing equally ill-fitting uniforms and sporting equally wide eyes, and saw that on the wall of our classroom hung a painting of an old man, looking as out of place in these 'modern' times as I felt in this new school environment. The wall he hung from faced a bank of windows, looking out from the high elevation of the school site, over Belfast, sprawling below, all war-torn and impoverished. I noticed that this old man seemed to look out the window and I was drawn to do the same. What did he see, this old man from a time gone by? And what did he mean me to see, now that I was part of a school community where his picture had pride of place in every room?

Edmund Ignatius Rice, the old man in the picture looking out of the window, was to have a profound effect on my life as a young boy from a working-class background in Belfast city. I was not the first such young boy, of course. Long before Edmund had looked out of that classroom window in Belfast in 1983, around the turn of the nineteenth century, he had looked out of a window in Waterford, prompted by the sister of the local bishop. Edmund was at a point of deep sadness in his life. He had lost his wife in a tragic accident and his daughter, born on the death bed of his wife, was born with profound disabilities. Edmund considered giving up his life in Ireland and going to a monastery in France. Perhaps it would be harsh with the gift of hindsight to say that he would have been running away, but it seems that the wise woman who orientated him to the window felt that he was. She encouraged him to open his eyes to what was there to be seen. What he saw that day changed his life utterly. He looked out and saw what has been described as a 'band of ragged boys'. Having been one such boy myself, I know the sight he would have looked out on! But 'looking out' and 'seeing' are two different things. Many look, but few truly see. That day, I believe, Edmund truly saw; he saw what God wanted him to see. Helped by the wise woman, he saw that running away was not an option – there was work to do at home. Already committed to supporting charities for the poor up to that point, Edmund, from that moment, changed direction in his life and intensified his work for the poor. This change of direction led to the establishment of schools to educate, nurture and feed the poor young people he saw, as well as the establishment of two religious orders in the fullness of time.

It is interesting for me that Edmund was given the name Ignatius as his middle name. Could he have been named for St Ignatius Loyola, the founder of the Society of Jesus – the Jesuits? St Ignatius is associated with a spirituality of seeing God in all things. I myself have written from an Ignatian

Foreword

perspective that we can find God in the mess of life. What Edmund saw that day in Waterford was God in the mess of life. He saw dignity and unrealised potential in the ragged band of boys. Importantly, and unlike St Ignatius whose spirituality has global and catechetical outworking, Edmund developed a spirituality that had a focus on practical poverty and on local problems and local solutions.

What would we see if we looked out our window through eyes of compassion as Edmund did so many years ago? What local problems and local solutions would they want us to discern as being the way forward? These questions will be explored in the pages of this book. The contributors will take us on a journey across the world and across many different pressing issues for our world today; from Maria Garvey exploring the care and giftedness of our sisters and brothers who are differently abled; to Lorna Gold writing for us about the care of our common home, the earth; to Brother Dennis Gleeson (one of the architects of this book) who opens our eyes to the need for our Church today to understand and live out of the spirituality of Edmund Ignatius Rice. Some contributors will have been directly influenced by Edmund in their education or vocation – others will not have been. However, all are gifted with what Edmund had: the ability not only to look out but also to see. Their insights will inform, console and challenge you as you read. Go with it and ask yourself how your view of the world and the part you have to play in it changes as you read.

I looked out of windows with Edmund in St Mary's for seven years. I have to be honest and tell you that when I left school, I could not have given chapter and verse on the details of his life. Having gotten to know him better now, I think he would have been happy enough with that. He never made it about him. What would also have pleased him, I think, is that I left school having experienced his spirituality – almost by osmosis – as I witnessed the emphasis placed on working for the poor and needy, on challenging systems that keep people down and the emphasis on our own responsibility for creating a better world.

I last looked out of a window as a pupil in St Mary's in June 1990. That day I stepped out into the world knowing much more than I did when I went in and having been challenged and resourced to live out my life inspired by the old man in the pictures on the walls, to continue to look out windows and wonder what God wanted us to see as the problems and solutions in what we saw. May this book itself be another window on the world for all who read it.

Acknowledgements

We are indebted to many people for bringing this project to fruition. In particular, we would wish to thank those who contributed to this book for their willingness to engage with the work, their co-operation, dedication and, of course, their patience.

We would also wish to thank the members of our advisory team – Aideen D'Arcy, Jim Deeds and Paddy Linden – for their wonderful support in shaping this work. Their wisdom, advice and encouragement have been invaluable.

We would like to take this opportunity to acknowledge and sincerely thank our colleagues in the Edmund Rice Network for all of their support and encouragement during this project. We would also wish to express our gratitude to numerous friends who have accompanied and journeyed with us throughout the writing of this work.

We also wish to pay particular gratitude to Pamela McLoughlin, Síne Quinn, David Macken and Padraig McCormack of Veritas for their support and guidance throughout the journey of bringing this work to completion. Finally, sincerest thanks to everyone at Veritas for their most professional support and expertise in the publication of this book.

All royalties from sales of this book will be directed to two charitable causes that have been supported by the Christian

Brothers and Edmund Rice Network over many years. They are Kabwata Orphanage in Lusaka, Zambia, and the Ruben Centre – specifically the Maternal and Child Health Support Programme – in Kibera township in Nairobi, Kenya.

Introduction

> For as worldly people love and seek with great diligence honour, fame and high reputation, so they who are spiritual and who seriously follow Christ love and ardently desire the things opposite to them.[1]

Those who dare to look at those in need through eyes of compassion and love are moved to act. So it was with Edmund Rice who, seeing the dire conditions in which so many impoverished young people were living in Waterford city, was called to respond. The plight of the poor was not only a catalyst for him to assist the needy in Waterford but it acted as a stark reminder of his own situation at that time. In his own brokenness, he was moved to recognise the brokenness of those in need around him and to act decisively with compassion.

The story of Edmund Rice looking out a window in Waterford more than two centuries ago is one that has been told to generations of people throughout the world who have had connections with the Christian Brothers and the Edmund Rice Network. This was a very dark and sorrowful time in Edmund's life. His young wife, Mary, had died in a tragic accident in 1789 while pregnant, and their daughter had been born prematurely and with special needs. So, looking through one broken window, which was the wreckage of his life, it is told that Edmund, on the brink of despair, was considering leaving his young daughter in the care of his step-sister, Joan Murphy, and going to Rome to enter an Augustinian monastery in order to dedicate his life to God through prayer and contemplation. Yet even at his lowest point, Edmund recognised that there were others also in need and chose not to follow that path. The story is that, as he looked out another window in Mary Power's house (his close friend John Power's sister), she challenged him to respond to the impoverished and excluded young people who were wandering aimlessly around the docks of Waterford city: 'Well, Mister Rice, while you go and bury yourself in a monastery, what will happen to these poor boys? Can't you do something for them?' The challenge was to recognise the same God-given beauty and dignity that he saw in his daughter in these ragged street urchins. So, inspired, perhaps, by his own daughter and certainly in response to the challenge by Mary Power, Edmund Rice decided to act.

Over the next number of years Edmund worked tirelessly to improve the conditions of those living in poverty and hopelessness. As a young boy, he would have had direct experience of the Penal Laws that (among many other things) excluded Catholics from education. Edmund Rice received his own education at a hedge school and would have appreciated the importance of education for the individual and the wider community. Yet, for Edmund, education was not simply a means of social advancement or individual escape to material wealth. Rather, he viewed education as simultaneously a sacred and secular activity, through which the dignity of the young would be enhanced and the humanisation of society would be advanced. Edmund Rice recognised that education would break the chains of poverty and bring the good news into the world – especially for the poor. He gave considerable financial support to the Presentation Sisters who opened a school for disadvantaged girls in Waterford in 1798. Inspired by their work, Edmund decided to follow their example and in 1802 set up a school in stable buildings in New Street for excluded and marginalised boys, such as those he had seen as he looked out of the window some years previously. And so the foundations of what has become the network of Christian Brothers' schools were laid. Today, some two centuries after Edmund Rice set up his first school in Waterford, there are Edmund Rice schools in more than twenty countries throughout the world, providing education to more than 170,000 students in Africa, North and South America, Australia, New Zealand and India, as well as in Ireland and England. Many of these young people would not be receiving an education if it had not been for a man who looked out of a window – saw, was moved and acted. Edmund's message of encouragement to Br Edward O'Flaherty in 1837 to 'have courage, the good seed will grow up in our children's hearts' has landed on fertile ground throughout the world today.

Dark clouds hover over the world – but light still breaks through
In the years since Edmund was moved to act, the world has changed enormously. The pace of change – especially in recent decades – has been quite bewildering. Advances in science, technology, medicine, industry, food production, knowledge, travel and communication, and in a host of other areas of life, have produced a global world in which nothing – or no one – exists in isolation or detached from others. We are at a crossroads in human living and the road to be taken has not been decided yet.

Of course, there are dangers and threats as well as opportunities. In his recent encyclical, *Fratelli Tutti*, Pope Francis warns of and reflects on the many distortions and challenges resulting from globalisation that threaten the development of our common humanity. These include the loss of the meaning of community, the culture of selfishness and indifference towards others and the common good, and the emergence of a 'throw-away' culture in which everything – including people themselves – is considered of value only in so far as it or they are deemed useful according to the dictates of the market. Our modern world is threatened by 'a culture of walls' in which humanity's fraternity and innate love for one another is lessened. For some, living for others has been replaced by living for self.[2]

Yet, despite all of these challenges and threats to authentic human living, we are constantly being made aware of our own vulnerability and need for community. In 2020 a pandemic struck the world, reminding us, in the cruellest way, of our interconnectedness. The world we knew as familiar and normal has been turned upside down by Covid-19, which has struck all of our lives like a tidal wave. However, even in these most challenging of times, we are a people of hope and light; we remain open to the Spirit who can inspire us to imagine anew. Through building a civilisation of love in which we see each and every person as a brother or sister – indeed, as God's very presence, as befitting one made in his image and likeness – all darkness and fear can be overcome.

Glimpses of a new possible world

> Were we to know the merit and value of only going from one street to another to serve a neighbour for the love of God, we should prize it more than Gold or Silver.[3]

In the Acts of the Apostles (chapters 1–2), we are told that following the ascension of Jesus to heaven, the disciples,

Introduction

confused and filled with fear, locked themselves away. In these uncertain times, we may feel like doing the same. Yet, Edmund Rice would not have been hiding like the early disciples – paralysed by fear before the Holy Spirit came on them. He looked into his heart and trusted in the Spirit for wisdom, guidance and courage in order to bring good news to those who were so desperately in need of it. He did not seek to start a world-wide schooling system or found a religious order. Motivated by a deep sense of compassion based on the gospel, he looked out the window in Waterford, saw the wretched condition of the young people in front of him, heard the cry of the poor and responded. He saw, judged and acted – the methodology that lies at the heart of living the social gospel. In so doing, he was pointing towards a new and different reality, based not on selfishness but on selflessness, not on power but on service, not on indifference or love of self but on care and compassion and love of the other. The world as it exists is not the only possible world. The 'culture of walls' can be replaced by a culture of compassion, love and fraternity. Edmund Rice's life and example demonstrates that an alternative way of living, based on the vision of a world founded on compassion and love, is achievable. It is in striving for this new world that the kingdom of God is created and God's will is done on earth as it is in heaven.

Contributions and contributors

This work is a sharing of this radical way of being by twenty people from a wide range of backgrounds and experiences throughout the world who did not allow themselves to be imprisoned by a 'culture of walls' but who dared to see, to judge and to act. In this book the reader will encounter a diverse range of passionate and talented contributors who – like Edmund Rice – looked out a window onto the world in which they found themselves and responded. The reader will encounter Edmund's vision of education in a number of contributions, including those by Pádraig Ó Fainín and Don O'Leary. Marist Brother Don Bisson, Darryl Cronin and Phil Glendenning remind us of the necessity of breaking down racial and ethnic barriers, while Sister Una Agnew and Maria Garvey respectively examine how society views the elderly and those living with disability and invite us to consider how we can learn from them. Father Peter McVerry, Brother Philip Pinto and Aidan Donaldson reflect on a God of compassion who calls us into the margins where we will encounter him in a most direct and special way. Brother Denis Gleeson considers the challenge of spiritual impoverishment for the world and Church today. Brother John McCourt outlines the remarkable struggle of the impoverished people of Zambia who persist in the face of great inequality, corruption and the ongoing HIV/AIDS pandemic. The threat to all of humanity – and especially the poor – through the destruction of creation is outlined in the clearest terms by Lorna Gold. Sister Sheila Curran explores new paths for the Church that focus on justice and integral ecology. Gladys Ganiel writes of the scandal of Christian division in Northern Ireland and of the courageous gospel witness of Fr Gerry Reynolds. Lesley O'Connor describes the courageous work of those involved in seeking to bring about reconciliation in Israel and Palestine. The reader will learn from Brother Martin Byrne of urban contextual theology and of God's presence in the North Wall area of inner-city Dublin. We are delighted to include in this work a contribution from of the most prominent lay Catholics in the world today and member of the Pontifical Council for Justice and Peace, Dr Michel Camdessus, who very kindly offered to this project his keynote address to the Down and Connor Faith and Life Convention, which he delivered in Belfast in September 2019.

This work also contains a foreword by Jim Deeds, writer, poet and catechist, and a postscript by Angela Miyanda, leading Zambian charity worker and director of Kabwata Orphanage in Lusaka.

Each of the contributors to this book raises important questions and issues, but what is most pertinent in this collection of writings is the collective sense of Edmund Rice's significant legacy and how we can continue to empower his vision. Their stories demonstrate the capacity to see one's fellow man and woman – and especially those in need – as a brother and sister and that compassion is a universal dimension that lies at the heart of every one of us and enables us to envisage and engender a new, open world. This is what Edmund did as a true disciple of Christ. This is what all who dare to call themselves followers of Christ are urged to do – to go into the world and announce the good news with joy wherever the Spirit leads us.

Endnotes

1 Edmund Rice, quoted in Desmond Rushe, *Edmund Rice: The Man and His Times*, Dublin: Gill and Macmillan, 1981, p. 124.
2 See Pope Francis, *Fratelli Tutti*, 18–21, 27.
3 Letter from Edmund Rice to Bryan Bolger, 1810, in Desmond Rushe, *Edmund Rice: The Man and His Times*, Dublin: Gill and Macmillan, 1995, p. 76.

MAKING GOD VISIBLE WHERE GOD SEEMS INVISIBLE

Philip Pinto

Any message that is not related to the liberation of the poor in a society is not Christ's message. Any theology that is indifferent to the theme of liberation is not Christian theology.[1]

Silence is the language of faith. Action – be it church or charity, politics or poetry – is the translation. As with any translation, action is a mere echo of its original, inevitably faded and distorted, especially as it moves farther from its source. There the comparison ends, though, for while it is true that action degrades that original silence, and your moments of meditative communion with God can seem a world away from the chaotic human encounters to which those moments compel you, it is also true that without these constant translations into action, that original, sustaining silence begins to be less powerful, and then less accessible, and then finally impossible.[2]

Edmund Rice, we are told, opened 'his whole heart to Christ present and appealing to him in the poor'.[3] That phrase has always resonated deeply with me. What does it mean to open one's *whole* heart? How does one open one's heart to anything? What is this presence of God in the poor? These are some of the questions I seek to address, because I believe that the answers to these questions lie at the core of what drives us to ministry with those on the margins.

In an honest and critical look at society in India today, social activist Harsh Mander writes, 'the paramount marker of the first decade of twenty-first-century India [is] the extraordinary indifference that people of privilege have for the intense and pervasive levels of human suffering all around them.'[4] He then quotes philosopher and public intellectual Noam Chomsky, who says: 'What is really striking to me … is the indifference of privileged sectors to the misery of others. You walk through Delhi and cannot miss it, but people just don't seem to see it. … they put themselves in a bubble and then they don't see it.'[5]

Two of the most formidable challenges facing our world in the twenty-first century are how governments of all countries will handle inequality and how they will deal with diversity. Both of these challenges describe the reality of our human relationships at this time in history. One has only to look at the suspicion with which we so often view the 'other'. Politicians and leaders across the board play on these fears and exacerbate polarisation between groups. More and more we are retreating into tribal mentalities, circling the wagons and keeping the others out.

Our modern world seems preoccupied with narrow self-interest driven by greed. Life is all about self: my needs, my comfort, my interests, my family and so on. Just consider some of the slogans and comments often heard today: 'Make America Great Again'; 'Take back control of our future'; 'Keep refugees out – and keep our values intact'; 'Keep Europe

Christian – Muslims out.' The advertising hoardings urge us to get more rather than be more. It is as if humanity has lost its moral compass. Fear and suspicion have taken over from compassion and kinship.

It is against this reality that the story of Edmund Rice makes such an impact. He was a member of the privileged section of society in his day. Yet, after the death of his wife, he was encouraged by a close friend, Mary Power, to notice the sufferings of the young boys of his city. Mary invited him to see the familiar scene with new eyes. The children that he passed each day on his way to and from work now took on a special identity. He now saw what others could not see: a common humanity. They were not separate from him; what affected them, affected him. As the Muslim poet and mystic Rumi said, 'If your eyes are open you will see the things worth seeing.' It is little wonder that the ability to see is so emphasised in the gospels. 'But blessed are your eyes, for they see, and your ears, for they hear' (Mt 13:16).

In a very perceptive reflection, the English rabbi Jonathan Sacks writes that the twin foundations on which Western culture was built were that of ancient Greece and ancient Israel. These two cultures were very different. The Greeks had a very visual culture and its greatest achievements were those dealing with seeing. Their art, architecture and glorification of the human body (through games and drama) were spectacles – performances that were seen. Plato imagined knowledge as a sort of vision underlying reality, seeing beneath the surface to the true form of things. And from here we get our dominant idea of knowledge as seeing: we speak of insight, hindsight, we adopt a perspective, we offer an observation, we shed light on a subject and we say 'I see' when we understand something.

Ancient Israel was different. It enjoined on its people the daily task of listening: 'Hear, O Israel: The Lord is our God, the Lord alone' (Deut 6:4); 'O that today you would listen to his voice! Do not harden not your hearts' (Ps 95:7-8). The injunction is to 'listen' to God's commandments. The Hebrew word for 'listen' has a very deep significance. It can be translated as 'to hear', 'to listen', 'to heed', 'to pay attention', 'to respond', to obey' and 'to understand'.[6] Listening ceases to be a passive activity but demands involvement and participation.

In a moment of mystical insight, Jesus said: 'Blessed are the eyes that see what you see! For I tell you that many prophets and kings desired to see what you see but did not see it and to hear what you hear but did not hear it' (Lk 10:23-4). Jesus was saying that his followers belonged to a new and radically different consciousness, a new way of seeing and hearing. His very first words recorded in the gospels are to a change of consciousness: 'The time is fulfilled, and the kingdom of God has come near; repent, and believe in the good news' (Mk 1:15). The Greek word for repent, *'metanoia'*, was not to feel sorry for one's sins – the God of the mystic's experience is not overly concerned about sin – but to allow oneself to be changed, to put on a new attitude, a new mind-set. Change your way of thinking if you wish to believe the Good News.

> Conversion is not an exercise in orthodoxy. Conversion is the heart-wringing process of becoming new – always and regularly and with exhausting consciousness. When we give ourselves to the process of conversion, day after long, long day, we give ourselves to the eternal moment of birth, of being new again. Otherwise we shall surely shrivel, fixed in a state of mind, a state of heart, a phase of life too small for us to breathe, to think, to be.[7]

The mystics, across the board, irrespective of religion, invite us to change our consciousness. Today, perhaps more than ever before, we are faced with a dire choice: change our consciousness or perish! This 'putting on' of a new mind is not like putting on a new shirt or a new pair of spectacles. This putting on costs us. It often tears us apart and turns us inside out. Falling in love with God turns one's world upside down. One cannot explain this, only experience it.

As the Persian Sufi poet Hafez said: 'I have learned so much from God that I can no longer call myself a Christian, a Hindu, a Muslim, a Buddhist, a Jew.' The old categories may no longer contain reality as we experience it. Once one is caught up in a new consciousness, life is forever changed.

And this is what happened to Edmund Rice as he looked out of the window. He was seeing with new eyes. His heart was stretched beyond its normal limits to take in the pain and the potential of the world. 'You can never discover how big the heart is until you are willing to let everything in. That's the astounding possibility of a human lifetime.'[8]

A new awareness of ourselves and our connection to the rest of creation enlarges our hearts and gives us the energy to do things we would not dream of otherwise. Every one of the writers in these pages has had an experience that grounded them in a new reality, a 'burning bush' moment. Sometimes it is a conscious experience; at other times it is a gradual opening of the eyes. It is this experience that gives them the energy and creativity that ministry to the margins thrives on. It is ever thus. Our tradition tells us that every such encounter with the life of the universe, the mystery we call God, carries with it the responsibility of making that encounter visible to others. Our ministry at the margins is nothing other than this: making God visible where he seems to be invisible.

Every human being experiences this encounter in some form or other, but most of us get distracted by the many calls of daily life and ignore what is happening. We allow the moment to pass and get on with our lives. The attentive soul is the one that allows transformation to take place. How does this happen?

I remember the Australian priest and missionary Fr Frank Andersen teaching the mantra: 'The wind will blow anywhere it will; we do not know where the wind will blow.' Where does the wind blow? One of the most dangerous places for the wind to blow is in our hearts! If we are attentive to the wind, our lives will never be the same again. Look at Moses. Look at Jesus of Nazareth. Look at Edmund Rice. Look at the many people who have paid attention to the wind's blowing – like the contributors in this book. Look at yourself.

The trouble with society today is that we do not go into the silence necessary to move into the quiet of our hearts. Our lives are too busy and too loud. Jesus invites us, 'Whenever you pray, go into your room [your heart] and shut the door and pray to your Father who is in secret; and your Father who sees in secret will reward you' (Mt 6:6). This is something that was a major part of Edmund's life, especially after his wife's death. Look at the number of spiritual practices that he undertook: reading the Bible, attending Mass, joining a number of pious associations and being involved in many charitable activities. All of this was slowly preparing him for the final decision that awaited him when he looked out of the window.

I believe that our gradual putting on of the mind of Jesus occurs when we sit in stillness with the impact human suffering has on our hearts. We cannot remain indifferent to what we see and hear. Our compassion is stirred to action. We are our brothers' and sisters' keepers!

As we read the different expressions of involvement with those on today's peripheries in the following chapters, try to recognise beneath the actions of generous people the way they have been able to see and to hear the cry of the poor. They are operating out of a different consciousness, a Jesus consciousness, that enables them to realise the other as truly brother and sister. They are no different from you or from me but for the fact that they have acted while we may choose to remain untouched and indifferent. As they share their stories, may all of us be encouraged to move out of our cocoons. We do this for our sake, for our transformation. This is not charity. This is living life fully. To look away from the plight of those in the margins and to close our ears to the cry of the poor is to ignore our brothers and sisters. It also is a denial of our own true humanity and a rejection of our own redemption and salvation.

Reflection
- *Philip Pinto reminds us that Edmund Rice did not just act differently but saw the world through a different lens – the lens of the heart, the lens of compassion, the lens of Jesus. And he listened differently too – and heard the cry of the poor.*
- *Do we allow ourselves to see and hear differently or do we just close our eyes and ears to those in need as we get on with our ever-busy private lives?*
- *Do we stop, look and listen and allow our hearts to be touched by the plight of our brothers and sisters in the margins?*
- *Do we make God visible in those places where he seems hidden yet is there waiting for us to see and encounter him?*

Endnotes

1. James H. Cone, *A Black Theology of Liberation,* New York: Orbis Books, 2010, p. ix.
2. Christian Wiman, *My Bright Abyss: Meditation of a Modern Disciple,* New York: Farrar, Straus and Giroux, 2013, p. 107.
3. Congregation of Christian Brothers, *Charism Statement,* Rome: Congregation of Christian Brothers, 1982.
4. Harsh Mander, *Looking Away: Inequality, Prejudice and Indifference in New India,* New Delphi: Speaking Tiger Books, 2015, p. 5.
5. Noam Chomsky, interviewed by Priyanka Borpujari, 'What is striking in India is the indifference of the privileged', *Tehelka,* 6 June 2013. Available at https://chomsky.info/20130706/; accessed 9 May 2022.
6. Jonathan Sacks, 'Listen, Really Listen – Eikev, 5778', Rabbisacks.org, 2 August 2018. Available at https://www.rabbisacks.org/covenant-conversation/eikev/listen-really-listen/; accessed 9 May 2022.
7. Joan Chittister, *There is a Season*, Oxford: Blackwell, 2005.
8. Gangaji, 'On Facing the Abyss', YouTube.com, 18 February 2014. Available at https://www.youtube.com/watch?v=XbQMPUJJ-VI; accessed 9 May 2022.

A WORLD AND A CHURCH SPIRITUALLY IMPOVERISHED

Denis Gleeson

Windows on a broken world
What do you see when you look through a window on the world today? Over two hundred years ago Edmund Rice, standing beside his friend Mary Power, looked through a window in Waterford and saw street children squabbling in the gutter. The Holy Spirit moved him to respond with compassion and he set about feeding, clothing and educating these children so that they could claim their dignity as human beings and choose to respond to the God in whose image they were made. For Edmund, therefore, education was not simply the ultimate response to poverty; it was the means by which people could begin to embrace their humanity and to realise their human and spiritual potential. It was, therefore, a path to conscious relationship with the Divine, personal transformation and the service of others. It was a path to growth, an acceptance of the fullness of the gift of life and an unfolding of the joy of the gospel.[1]

A spiritually impoverished world
Because of his openness to the promptings of the Holy Spirit, Edmund touched countless lives and challenges us, today, to

do the same. So when we look out a window, what do we see? The windows on our world today are provided by television newscasts and social media platforms. They show us a world of fabulous wealth and dire poverty; food surpluses and biblical famines; nations advanced in technology and nations that cannot provide sanitation or clean water for their people. They show us a world built on greed and self-interest, where the rights of individuals supersede the common good. It is a world where spiritual impoverishment produces moral indifference and economic and political paralysis. We seem incapable of resolving issues around homelessness in our cities, never mind responding adequately to global economic inequality. Developing nations can, inexplicably, spend more on armaments than on food programmes or the provision of shelter and basic services. Then, our ecological and environmental brinkmanship is further testament to the blindness that results from our seeming lack of moral focus and our dulled, blunted collective conscience.[2] Given our arrogance and spiritual self-neglect, even the Covid-19 pandemic might not lead us to change our ways.

For these reasons, I believe that the present level of spiritual impoverishment is what would distress Edmund most today because it is that type of impoverishment that sustains greed, self-interest, materialism and apparent apathy towards the plight of our neighbours. Spiritual impoverishment is at the root of our global inequality and that inequality, in turn, is at the root of all our social ills – national and international.[3] American theologian Fr Thomas Keating writes:

> The spiritually poor are those who lack the greatest resource of all, which is the conviction of God's presence within them as a loving God, healing their emotional and mental wounds, and inviting them to

share the divine life, light and love. This is where true happiness is.[4]

A spiritually impoverished Church
Spiritual impoverishment also feeds the inability, among many of us who profess to be Christians, to take in a gospel message which is all about our relationship with God and how that manifests in our relationships with each other. Our treatment of other people always remains the measure of our spiritual health. Does the Church always put relationships first, for example, when dealing with allegations of abuse? Sadly, the answer is that it does not and continuing and further unpardonable suffering is the result. Too often we practice a Christianity that functions at a remove from the gospel itself. When did we last hear a priest struggle with the Beatitudes in the pulpit? What do we think of the Beatitudes outlined by Pope Francis in 2016?[5] Were we even aware that he had spoken on the Beatitudes? Were they discussed and debated upon in our parishes? Did any action or changes result from this discussion? Do we, in fact, have any kind of serious interaction on the Christian message in our parishes?

We are not being nourished on a Sunday. There is little by way of encouragement and we are not being challenged in a positive and meaningful manner. Pope Francis could hardly put it more forcefully when he writes:

> In some people we see an ostentatious preoccupation for the liturgy, for doctrine and for the Church's prestige, but without any concern that the Gospel have a real impact on God's faithful people and the concrete needs of the present time.[6]

Yet, our liturgy is the most amazing gift when it is inclusive in all respects. It can raise the spirits with music. It can comfort and calm with silence. It can inform and motivate with well-chosen readings. It can inspire with well-chosen words and move us to action and service. It can facilitate our celebration, accommodate our transitions in life, heal us and forgive us when we wound and are wounded and it can ritualise, solemnly and with dignity, our grieving and our letting go when we are bereaved. But good liturgies are not easily come by and opportunities to touch and even transform people's lives are routinely squandered.

It was a friend, Mary Power, who challenged Edmund and gave him his way forward. So, imagine, for example, the kind of Church we might have if women were allowed to have a voice and to participate fully? Conversations like that between Jesus and the woman at the well could be ongoing even now. How that would enrich us! Full inclusion and 'a more incisive female presence' in both Church and society would allow the sensitivity, insight and compassion of modern women to become creatively and wonderfully contagious.[7] Full inclusion, in fact, of all laypeople in the Church would dramatically renew the Church and re-energise it. It would provide a much-needed antidote to the 'excessive clericalism' Pope Francis has complained of.[8]

We will, therefore, have to begin investing more in people than we do in buildings. If laypeople are to serve as lay ministers they must be properly prepared for the roles they will play. However, there appears to be little sign of such preparation being offered on the scale that is needed and to the standard that is required. This is both tragic and actually sinful because it is a rejection of what is clearly a movement of the Spirit. It is a refusal to grow and an infliction upon ourselves of unnecessary suffering.

Our Church remains a sinful church. We have failed people in so many ways. The legacy of a brand of theological, spiritual, moral and liturgical persecution that was widespread in the past still weighs heavily upon us. Pope Francis has, for example, found it necessary to remind priests that 'the confessional must not be a torture chamber'.[9] These are startling words. Again, the elderly can still fret about not observing days of fasting and abstinence or about missing Mass on a Sunday. Conscientious and devout parents can worry that God loves their adult children less because they no longer attend church regularly. Worse still, adherence to outdated theologies threatens to deprive people of an understanding of the deeper dimensions of life and even undermines intimacy with the Divine itself.

Negative, destructive images of God are sometimes reinforced rather than challenged and the 'Abba' that Jesus revealed, the God of love, the God who longs to engage intimately with us as a Father, is pushed into the background. Negative and distorted images of God are a major issue for so many people and this impoverishes us all. Our God is a great, expansive, generous, inventive, forgiving and open-handed God and there can be no ambivalence about that. We can gaze, of course, in awe, but there is no place today for a theology, or a spirituality, that is tainted by fear or accommodates violence to oneself or others.

The same applies, in the moral arena, where Church guidance has frequently been lacking the vital ingredient of Jesus' gospel, which is compassion. In addition, there has not been clear and consistent confirmation of the critical role always played by informed, individual conscience. Even now, contraception remains the classic instance of this. The result is that sincere and committed people are left disturbed, disenchanted and suffering unnecessarily. Moral leadership has been rare, as has a willingness to engage in dialogue in the public forum. This despite the major contributions made by Pope Francis in recent years and the humble and courageous example he has given.

A Church and a world without good news?

Too often, the gospel that the Church proclaims is simply not good news and is not a gospel of joy. The Pope says that: 'It is undeniable that many people feel disillusioned and no longer identify with the Catholic tradition.'[10] He adds that our institutions have failed to be genuinely welcoming. Most devastating, however, is his observation that pastoral care, especially among the poor, leaves much to be desired and that 'the worst discrimination which the poor suffer is the lack of spiritual care.'[11] These words are astounding. We cannot but be shocked and shamed by them. How did such a state of affairs come to pass? Sadly, I believe the explanation is that we are not sufficiently grounded in the gospel itself to appreciate, in full, the demand to serve and the joy that such service can bring.

Actually, in the Catholic tradition, we are not familiar enough with the scriptures as a whole. We do not know how to read the scriptures and, by and large, we are oblivious to the rich insights of modern biblical scholarship. In fact, the interpretation of scripture that we receive from the pulpit at times verges on the fundamentalist, and this short changes loyal church congregations. Every churchgoer should know, at least, of the useful and ancient allegorical approach to scripture. Pope Francis is uncompromising concerning the sacred writings when he says that: 'The study of the sacred Scriptures must be a door opened to every believer.'[12] Every churchgoer, therefore, should be familiar with *lectio divina*, which can feed into discursive meditation and centring prayer, but where is the evidence that we are applying ourselves to this task?

In addition to the opportunity to study the scriptures, every churchgoer should have the option of access, at least on occasion, not just to the sacrament of reconciliation but to professional spiritual accompaniment. More than ever we need to experience, in a fresh and contemporary way, our extensive and ancient contemplative tradition. We need a Church that can approach the Father in receptive silence, that can listen intelligently to the Word in the gospel and that can respond with freedom and creativity to the invitation of the Holy Spirit to reach out to others in service. These are the means by which we can stand beside Edmund and look out the window on the contemporary world. To build a Church that will respond to all who are impoverished we need honesty, discernment, a vision informed by scripture, a contemplative stance and a committed community. It will not happen on its own. We need experienced spiritual facilitators. We need prophetic voices. We need leadership, generative conversation and humility.

The question is, when the Pope provides such leadership and is a prophetic voice in the Church, are we really listening? *Laudato Si'* is a magnificent document that could hardly have been more timely or more relevant. Yet, what was its reception like in local parishes? Were free copies given out in every church? Was it enthusiastically proclaimed? Were child- and adolescent-friendly summaries generated? Were people encouraged to take action, even within their own homes and their own communities? These are fair and legitimate questions that are deserving of more than a little consideration. Climate change, after all, is one of the critical issues of our time and the feebleness of our response to it, both within Church and society, says much about our spiritual impoverishment and our estrangement from a God who holds all of life in being.

A contemplative stance and the universe within

The God that we worship today cannot remain a God 'out there' beyond the stars, a passive and distant God, a God removed from life and residing in the heavens beyond. Our God today must be the God of the scriptures, the God within, the God who reaches out to Abraham, Sarah, and each of us, seeking relationship and intimacy. Our God is a God who searches the heart rather than monitors behaviour. We should never tire of proclaiming a God of boundless love and mercy. Again, ours is a great God, who gifts us life with generosity and abundance and whose incarnate Word came to embrace humanity and to heal, to free and to enlighten.

In the gospel, Jesus proclaims a God who is 'Abba', Father. Moreover, the good news that Jesus confirms for us about 'Abba' is that God is love, that God is in all of life and that the fullness of human life can be found only in God. For Jesus, there can be no barriers between us and God. That is why he cleansed the temple of its money-driven sacrificial practices. They were proving a barrier between God and ordinary people as they sometimes smacked of attempts to buy favour with God. This angered Jesus because God is always present to us. In fact, the only thing that can separate us from God is the thought that we are separate from God.[13] Now, if only we could lose that thought, what a difference it would make to us and to all whose lives touch ours. As I have said, our service of others is a measure of our spiritual health and our relationship with the Divine. Our spiritual growth, however, poses a further key question on our spiritual journey. This question is not about how holy we have become, or at what stage of development we are at in our prayer life; it is about how far we are prepared to trust God. This is what faith basically comes down to. It is always, in some form or other, a matter of trust.

In the maelstrom of life, it takes courage to trust in God and to lead our lives only with a view to his son, Jesus. At times, we cry out with the apostles on the stormy sea of Galilee, 'Teacher, do you not care that we are perishing?' (Mk 4:38). In the gospel story, Jesus' response is to tell the wind and to sea, 'Peace! Be still!' (39). Then, as the waters become calm, Jesus turns to his apostles and asks them 'Why are you afraid?' (40). It is a question we all face. Perhaps the answer lies in learning to obey Jesus' command to the wind and waves, 'Peace! Be still!' The responses we need for the various crises we face in life will only arise from the depths of our truest being when we engage with silence. To do this we must dramatically broaden our definition of prayer. Reading or writing, talking or singing, preparing a meal or walking in the park must all become prayer-privileged moments when we can experience silence and learn to listen to what is going on within ourselves and around us.

Taking a contemplative stance in life connects us to the divine energy that fuels all of creation. In contrast to the compulsive distractedness that characterises many of our days, it is through silence and stillness that our lives actually get real. The more we engage fully with others in our ministry and in the sharing of the spiritual, the more human and the more real we become. We become ourselves through our giving of ourselves. After quiet attentiveness to the Holy Spirit within, we can give wholehearted service to all we meet. Intimacy with the Father, Abba, and the offer of healing service to all he encountered were the hallmarks of Jesus' life on earth. If we are to live by any other standard we will remain impoverished spiritually.

Jesus was also very much a social being. He loved to gather people around him. He enjoyed a celebration. He liked to share a meal with whoever would share with him and actually told us to remember him in the breaking of the bread. His sharing of loaves and fishes with those who followed him was marked by generosity, inclusion and abundance. His last supper with his closest disciples was a final giving of himself. It was preceded by a hugely symbolic act of service: the washing of the feet of all those in attendance. How all of this contrasts with the impoverished nature of much of what we experience as Sunday Eucharist, where people sit passively, are sometimes excluded from Communion, though they crave to receive, and where joy, abundance, communal inclusion and generosity are often sadly lacking. Have we forgotten that the Lord delights greatly in us and rejoices over us with singing?[14]

Still, there is always hope, and within both Church and society, there are many people of goodwill and the Spirit is always at work.[15] Mutual respect, the acknowledgement of human dignity, a fairer society and a more peaceful world are not beyond us.[16]

Conclusion

Our way forward will have to be premised upon a more 'healthy pluralism,' where religion acknowledges civil authority's legislative obligations and where civil authority does not try to marginalise, denigrate or silence the voices of the great faith traditions.[17] These voices must be loud and clear and speak not for themselves but for all those who are silenced, powerless, suppressed and forgotten.

So, on a planet beset by global economic injustice and crushing poverty, Pope Francis challenges all of us that if we are to go beyond 'something more than a few sporadic acts of generosity', we must presume 'the creation of a new mindset which thinks in terms of community and the priority of the life of all over the appropriation of goods by a few.'[18] This calls for a seismic adjustment in the global economy and an acceptance that those who are privileged have an indisputable obligation towards the common good. We must finally begin to live up to that obligation. The rights and dignity of the poorest among us are real and extend far beyond mere inclusion in a United Nations charter. We must plumb the spiritual depths within us, both personally and collectively, if we are to find the courage, the will and the invention to meet such a challenge. It can be done.

Our experience of the Covid-19 pandemic, for example, provides a dramatic and cruel reminder of our blindness and limitations and the inequality in our world. Yet, it also heroically and emphatically illustrates for us that our future lies not in materialism, self-interest, individualism, nationalism and isolationism but in a shared search for meaning, in the communal, in service and in the relational. Are these lessons that we have taken on board as we stand beside Edmund looking out on our twenty-first century world? Surely, they have to be, or we will end so spiritually impoverished that we will look out through broken windows on our world and will not be able to see its beauty.

Reflection
- *What do you think of the claim that humanity's indifference and inability in the face of global problems like climate change and world poverty is due to spiritual impoverishment and that even the Church itself functions at a remove from the gospel?*
- *Do you agree with Pope Francis that too often the Church does not extend a welcome to people and that, shockingly, the poor lack spiritual care? What are the ways forward for both the world and the Church that are offered in this chapter?*

- *Are we boxed in and trapped by our social, economic and political structures? Are the poor and disadvantaged fated to remain poor and disadvantaged in our world?*

Endnotes

1 Cf. Pope Francis, *Evangelii Gaudium*, 2013, 1.
2 Cf. ibid., 2.
3 Cf. ibid., 202.
4 Thomas Keating, in T. Keating, L. Verboven and J. Boyle, *World Without End*, New York: Bloomsbury, 2017, p. 19.
5 Cf. Pope Francis, Homily at the Swedbank Stadium in Malmo, Sweden, 1 November 2016.
6 Pope Francis, *Evangelii Gaudium*, 95.
7 Ibid., 103.
8 Ibid., 102.
9 Ibid., 44.
10 Ibid., 70.
11 Ibid., 200.
12 Ibid., 175.
13 See Thomas Keating, *Foundations for Centering Prayer and the Christian Contemplative Life*, New York: Bloomsbury, 2002, p. 41.
14 Cf. Zeph 3:17.
15 Cf. *Evangelii Gaudium*, 178.
16 Cf. ibid., 180.
17 Ibid., 255.
18 Ibid., 188.

A WINDOW ON 2020: A YEAR OF CONVERGING CRISES

Lorna Gold

In early 2020 a terrifying crisis gripped the whole world, wreaking death and destruction as it spread out of control. The crisis spread with devastating speed, consuming everything in its path. We all watched on helplessly as countless lives were torn apart, as brave souls risked life and limb to protect their neighbours and salvage what they could. The scenes we witnessed seemed like something out of a Hollywood movie – except this was real life. The crisis I am talking about had nothing to do with the coronavirus. I am referring to the massive wildfires that spread across Australia, Indonesia, the Amazon and other parts of the world in the early months of 2020. These unprecedented fires, like the other climate-related emergencies that preceded them in the past few years, shook us all, at least for a short while. Nature seemed to be shouting out to us: 'Act now or the world could literally go up in flames!'

For three decades, climate scientists have been warning that emissions are continuing to rise and we are reaching a point of no return when it comes to our climate and ecological emergency. In 2019 many governments finally seemed to be willing to accept the urgency of the science and declared climate emergencies. The declarations were made –

'this is an emergency' – yet, bizarrely, nothing happened. Despite the impact on the poor and the fate of our children and grandchildren being in the balance, the disruption to normality would be far too much to contemplate. There were no solemn statements from our prime ministers on live, national TV. There were no dramatic measures to lower our emissions. It seems that no one seemed to know or remember what exactly a declaration of emergency meant. These were emergencies in name only. A normality of sorts prevailed.

Despite appearances, however, the momentum for change has been peeling away at that normality for years. In September 2019, the largest climate mobilisation in history called on governments to take the climate crisis seriously and protect the rights of future generations. Young people, and many adults, filled the streets of every city calling for urgent change. They called for the climate crisis to be treated as the emergency that it really is. Back in September 2019, for those engaged in protests, it must have felt like the tipping point – the wake-up call was finally being heard and people were starting to take action.

Together with other youth leaders, Greta Thunberg addressed the United Nations and outlined the urgency and the scale of the challenge we are facing. She spoke with passion and anger: 'You say you hear us and that you understand the urgency. But no matter how sad and angry I am, I do not want to believe that. Because if you really understood the situation and still kept on failing to act, then you would be evil. And that I refuse to believe.'[1] She echoed what 99 per cent of scientists have been saying for thirty years: that the world needs to bend the curve of emissions downwards with urgency. It requires us to dramatically shift how we live, work and think. And yet her words seemed to fall on deaf ears. The sheer inertia of the system seemed stuck in normality.

Then came the virus
The embers of those wildfires were still smouldering when the tiny, microscopic novel coronavirus SARS-CoV-2 jumped species in Asia, facilitated by human disregard for and destruction of nature. It started spreading across countries – carried by the wings of aeroplanes rather than birds. Our relentless drive to be on the go, our non-stop global society now became the super spreader of this new, deadly disease. Silently, the virus wielded its deadly power by weaponising gestures meant to show love: a kiss, a hug, a handshake, a caress, a simple touch. It spread through invisible droplets in the air – turning the exhale of one into a potentially a lethal dose for another. What long felt like empty space to us (air) suddenly seemed heavy. Air was invisible, yes, but teeming with particles we need to survive and ones that could harm us or our loved ones.

The virus arrived so dramatically, so unexpectedly, that it punched a hole in our consciousness. All of a sudden, the images of raging wildfires and silently melting ice sheets on our planet became a distant memory. Instead, our TVs and smartphones were filled with new images of apocalyptic scenes – first in faraway China, where the government was locking down cities and hospitals were struggling to cope with this new disease. Then we watched as sleepy Bergamo in northern Italy, with its snow-capped peaks, woke to find itself overwhelmed by people struggling to breathe. The nightmare then landed on our own shores. We knew that unless we acted urgently, for the greater good, many would die, especially among the old and the vulnerable.

Once we understood, we looked to our leaders and held our breath. Would they do the right thing? On what basis would they make decisions? Would they act like this was a *real* emergency or just another inconvenient truth in the way of profits? The responses from many – if not most – governments in the face of this emergency have been dramatic to say the least. This has, of course, exposed many problems and inconsistencies in our capacity to respond to these types of emergencies, but what is interesting and surprising is what the vast majority of governments did not do.

Whilst many governments initially delayed in taking robust measures, perhaps not grasping the full extent of the situation, one thing that governments by and large did not do as the virus emerged was to 'leave it to the market' and corporations to sort out. This could have easily been expected. 'Leaving it to the market' would have meant continuing the policy priorities that have dominated normal life for at least thirty years or more. It would have put the continuity of profits and the economy over the lives of the sick and vulnerable.

This is exactly what governments have done in relation to other emergencies, especially in relation to climate change. The protection of hedge funds, billionaires and oil companies has been treated as more important than the need to scale back or dramatically change industrial production to reduce carbon emissions. The fear of the state 'interfering' in the natural mechanisms of the free market and causing serious disruption to the economy hindered any significant intervention. These ideas that have dominated economic thinking, politics and public policy for at least the last thirty years.

Shared purpose rediscovered

In the face of the Covid-19 emergency, however, 'leaving it to the market' suddenly seemed the most foolish act. Even worse, such an act would be a dereliction of duty, a grotesque act, inhumane, utterly reckless, ludicrous. Though it had once seemed that the market was all that mattered and that there was 'no such thing as society', as Margaret Thatcher famously quipped, society all at once seemed the most important thing we had. Very early on it seemed that governments could see that the response to the threat of this virus and the impact it would have on large numbers of people, potentially infecting most of the world, required something different to a profit-motivated approach.

It required thoughtful, concerted collaboration between people taking decisions based on a renewed belief in a shared humanity. It required input from a great variety of professions rooted in the truth of the situation – from scientists to medical doctors, to behavioural psychologists, as well as a factual, trustworthy media. The distance between spin, fake news, half-truth and truth, which has often seemed blurred in recent times, became a matter of life and death. It required entire populations to come on board and change their lifestyles dramatically, with no timeline for when things might get back to normal. It required trust in the collective action of everyone to achieve something which nobody could achieve on their own: *to fight the virus by bending the curve of infections downwards.* We were all invited to find our part in this new story and to get to work for a common purpose, for the greater good.

In the midst of this crisis, we remembered things about ourselves that had perhaps become overshadowed by the frenetic pace of modern life and the constant messaging of a consumer society. We refocused our lives, slowed down and re-prioritised. In this new, slower world, we noticed and appreciated the small things on our daily walks in whatever green patches we could access. We became more appreciative of what it means to be alive. The pandemic also cast light on the dramatic inequality that pervades our societies, which meant that many of the essential workers on the front line lacked protection and were underpaid, and many people struggled to feed themselves and their families. Moreover, home did not offer safety to shelter in during the pandemic for all. Domestic violence soared.

Indian author Arundhati Roy perhaps best captured this dramatic break when she spoke of the pandemic being a portal.[2] As in other eras, the threat of infection forced us to *invent a whole new normal* for ourselves overnight out of what remained possible and safe. The invisible connections between us became as clear as day. Our need for friendship, contact and connection became as visceral as thirst and hunger. We felt driven to reach out and find ways to connect with and help others, to ease pain, to bring hope. At times, despite the pain and darkness, the pandemic gave way to a new kind of competitiveness: one of acts of kindness and compassion. This renewal of humanity was rooted in the knowledge that somewhere others were risking everything for us. Through this crisis, despite the confusion and many mistakes, humanity re-discovered a deeper truth: that for the most part, far from being evil (as Greta refused to believe), we have wells of compassion and solidarity that have perhaps gone unnoticed for a long time.

And nature breathed
As we focused on tackling this virus by slowing down and staying put, an unexpected miracle happened: the earth began to breathe again. Climate scientists told us for years that to cause catastrophic climate change we didn't need to do anything dramatic, we just needed to keep doing exactly what we were doing. By being 'normal' we were killing the planet. It was our normal life – particularly that of wealthier countries – that was causing climate change and pollution. But suddenly our endless air travel, extravagant lifestyles,

addiction to consumerism, industrial processes filling the air with pollution and many of our wasteful habits had to stop.[3] And the planet started to heal. During the first lockdown of 2020, carbon emissions dropped by over 5 per cent – an unprecedented drop, unseen since the Second World War.[4] Subsequent confinements would continue to flatline emissions during the pandemic.

Bending the curve of the coronavirus inadvertently started to bend the climate curve too. The pandemic bought us a precious window of time where the planet was not hurtling full speed towards the cliff of ecological destruction. In the words of the climate campaigners, the virus 'pulled the emergency break' that citizens and governments, even with massive campaigns on the streets, were unable to realise.

Choosing a new normal
Yet as the pandemic continues, and indeed intensifies in many parts of the world, we are already facing a dramatic choice in terms of the future of humanity and the planet. Emergency measures like lockdowns were only ever designed to be temporary. The whole world cannot remain in confinement forever. The suffering and pain of this situation could only grow the longer the strict measures were kept in place. As the Covid-19 pandemic worsened, it revealed much about the fragile nature of our political and economic systems. The UN drew attention to the compounding effect the coronavirus was having on other crises, such as famine outbreaks in parts of Africa caused by prolonged drought and locust plagues.[5] If world fails to respond as these crises as they emerge, the results could be catastrophic.

The reality is that the world is sitting at a fork in the road. It is becoming clear that the pandemic is *a crisis within a plethora of crises* and needs to be seen as such. We have to constantly remind ourselves that the old normal we knew before the pandemic was killing the planet and was far from a good normal. Tackling the acute crisis of the pandemic puts huge pressure on governments to recover economically and, of course, pay for all the additional spending that stopping the pandemic has involved. As governments seek to put together packages to promote recovery, we need to think about bail outs that address the roots of many crises – both socially just and green.

The big question, of course, is who pays? Taxes will have to increase to pay off the debts we have taken on. This crisis has shown us that those who are on the front line of our societies and vital to our survival are paid very little and lack security of employment. They need to be recognised for their sacrifice – and they need to be paid a lot more. The burden of *who pays* needs to address the massive inequality in our countries and in the world at large. Those with the broadest shoulders need to pay most. This should apply both within countries and between countries. Countries need to find ways to close all the loopholes that mean that large corporations and billionaires (especially those who have benefited from the pandemic) can avoid paying taxes, collaborate on tax havens and generate taxes on international finance. The time has come to address the massive inequality by ensuring that those who can pay do.

At the same time, the rescue packages need to be green – they need to factor in the opportunity the virus has given us to generate a new, low-carbon economy rather than propping up an old economy. This is about more than putting in place a few extra-wide cycle paths. What sense does it make to prop up oil prices when there is ample potential to move rapidly towards renewables? Rescue packages need to pro-actively support the structural changes needed to tackle climate change, such as the emergence of those sectors of the economy where there are green jobs, nature-based solutions and community solutions. We have so many solutions to the climate crisis – circular economy, renewable energy, sharing and solidarity economies. Through the Covid-19 pandemic, many of these have come to the forefront as a necessity.

Lessons of hope
If the pandemic is indeed a portal, each of us is on a journey through the old, the now and into the new of how we live our lives. As individuals, as families, as communities we are re-evaluating so much as our normal has been disrupted. Yet the challenge will be in translating what we have learned from the virus response into the bigger crisis of tackling climate emergency with the same sense of urgency and willingness to re-learn our normal.

Yet, through the crisis, there is more than a glimmer of hope. We have a once-in-a-generation, perhaps once-in-a-century, opportunity tell ourselves a new story that we have *lived through*. We may be experiencing this new story in very different ways, but it is a defining example of what it means to be human, about what we cherish and what we want to protect once everything is stripped back.

As Rabbi Johnathan Sacks said in relation to the pandemic:

> Here, we suddenly see our vulnerability. We've been coasting along for more than half a century in an unprecedented affluence, unprecedented freedom, unprecedented optimism. And all of a sudden we are facing the fragility and vulnerability of the human situation. And at the end of the day, even without a faith in God, we have to say either we work together and survive, or we work separately and perish. … A

revelation of the inescapably interlinked nature of our humanity.[6]

This echoes what Naomi Klein, author and activist, said in relation to the root of the climate crisis: 'We ... must undergo a radical revolution of values. We must rapidly begin the shift from a thing-orientated society to a person-orientated society.'[7] Is this not exactly what the pandemic has done – and continues to do – to us? This new awareness of our shared vulnerability and our shared future on one planet must now become the foundation of our 'new normal'.

Conclusion
As this book goes to print, we are still in the middle of the pandemic – and one thing this has taught us is that we cannot predict what comes next. The pandemic could be a temporary parenthesis in our failure to tackle the climate emergency, or it could be a turning point in the story. It could be a small downward bend in a relentless upward curve, or it could be the tipping point that leads to more dramatic changes in our society. The choice of what happens next will rest on the governments of the world coming together – but it ultimately will rest with the will of every citizen on the planet who makes choices every day, and who chooses those leaders. This virus has opened a crack in a window to see a slower world where we value consumer goods less and people and nature more. It has taught us that we are not evil, selfish automatons. We are interconnected and interwoven and, with huge sacrifices, together we can bend impossible curves. In doing so, through the despair, the virus has perhaps given us the greatest hope for a brighter future.

Reflection
- *The Covid-19 pandemic which caused so much devastation on a global scale is rightly regarded as a 'crisis for humankind'. Yet, as Lorna Gold points out, it should not be viewed as an isolated phenomenon or occurrence. Rather, the pandemic should be understood as part of a 'convergence of interconnected crises' (including the environmental crisis) which are the inevitable and direct result of the embracing of a destructive and unsustainable lifestyle based on consumerism, greed and individualism. Lorna Gold points out that the only true solution to these crises will come about when humanity – as a collective 'we' (and not simply a collection of 'egos') – realises the interconnectivity of all of its members (and with the environment) and refocuses how we live with one another and God's creation*
- *Will justice, economic re-balancing and human dignity be part of the overcoming of Covid-19 or will the poor be placed at the back of the queue as society begins to recover?*
- *Has the determination to tackle the environmental crisis become another victim of the pandemic?*
- *Edmund Rice dared to imagine a different world founded on compassion, love and service – a world stood upside down. Dare we imagine a different way of living for one another and not just self? Dare we imagine a 'new normal' or will we just go back to the 'old normal' which gave us the pandemic in the first place?*

Endnotes

1. 'Transcript: Greta Thunberg's Speech at the U.N. Climate Action Summit', NPR.org, 23 September 2019. Available at https://www.npr.org/2019/09/23/763452863/transcript-greta-thunbergs-speech-at-the-un-climate-action-summit; accessed 12 May 2021.

2. Arundhati Roy, 'The Pandemic is a Portal', *Financial Times*, 3 April 2020. Available at https://www.ft.com/content/10d8f5e8-74eb-11ea-95fe-fcd274e920ca; accessed 13 May 2022.

3. There is evidence, however, that the pandemic saw an unprecedented increase in disposable items associated with medical supplies and protection equipment, as well as a return to disposable plastic for everyday consumption.

4. Corinne Le Quéré et al., 'Temporary reduction in daily global CO2 emissions during the COVID-19 forced confinement', *Nature Climate Change*, Vol. 10, No. 7 (2020), pp. 647–53.

5. 'New wave of famine could sweep the globe, overwhelming nations already weakened by years of conflict, warn UN officials', *UN News*, 18 September 2020. Available at https://news.un.org/en/story/2020/09/1072712; accessed 13 May 2022.

6. Johnathan Sacks, interviewed by Emily Maitlis, 'The Pandemic will Fundamentally Change our Character and our Generation', RabbiSacks.org, 17 March 2020. Available at https://rabbisacks.org/rabbi-sacks-on-the-coronavirus-pandemic-extended-newsnight-interview/; accessed 13 May 2022.

7. Naomi Klein, *This Changes Everything – Capitalism vs. the Climate*, New York: Penguin Books, 2014, p. 38.

WORKING WITH THE POOREST AND THE FINEST: 'WE ARE WHAT WE ARE'

Pádraig Ó Fainín

'We are what we are.' I always thought this was a rather strange phrase. Sure, what else could we be? I suppose, though, what the phrase implies is that we are what we are as a result of what we've done, what we've experienced, our background, our rearing, nature and nurture, the sights and sounds and influences that have shaped us and therefore made into us what we are.

Sometimes I ponder how I ended up here; who I am, what I am – working with and amongst street children. These deprived children – hungry, dirty, poorly-dressed – are officially referred to by the Zambian authorities as 'Orphans and Vulnerable Children' (OVCs). This term hides a lot of misery in it. These young people who are labelled as OVCs are indeed neglected, forgotten, marginalised and dismissed by mainstream society but they are children and the best of children nonetheless. I suppose if you were to ask why, the answer is, of course, easy: 'we are what we are'.

From Waterford to Kabwe
I was born and reared in Waterford, growing up in the shadow of Mount Sion. I attended school in Mount Sion

just as my father did. Likewise, my grandfather, great-grandfather and probably beyond that again. It is no great leap of imagination to suggest that many of my direct relatives walked the corridors of Mount Sion, walked the streets and quays of Waterford, some perhaps even rubbing shoulders with Brother Edmund Ignatius Rice – and in all probability educated, fed and clothed by him. Like most other Waterford people, I grew up with the stories of Brother Rice working with and for the poorest of Waterford's poor. Our images were of bakers baking, tailors tailoring and teachers teaching. From an early age, we Waterfordians could tell you the life story of Brother Rice – about the prosperous man who gave it all away, a man who, ahead of his time, saw education as a basic human right, and about the difference he made to the lives of the 'poorest of the poor'. We could recite the Edmund Rice Prayer (the old version!) by heart: 'Oh God, who in thy love for the souls of innocent children …'

Let me put your mind at rest at once: I'm no Edmund Rice. I have no doubt, however, that somehow, somewhere deep in my psyche, Edmund Rice's story is what has prompted or persuaded or provoked me into action and has pushed or dragged or led me to where I am today, to the dirty, grimy, bustling town of Kabwe. It is a place in some ways, despite the geographical distance and passage of time, not unlike the Waterford of Edmund Rice. In Kabwe, Brother Rice is still having an effect. Indeed, we are what we are.

Makululu – a place abandoned
Makululu is a sprawling compound on the edge of town.[1] It is home to God knows how many people, with estimates varying from thirty thousand to ninety thousand living there. Maybe God himself doesn't even know, as it often seems to

me that Makululu has been forgotten by both man and God. It is not a pretty place – broken down shacks; a dust bowl in the searing heat of October, a river of mud and festering cholera black-spot in the rains; a sea of humanity, beaten down, hungry, uneducated humanity, no matter what the season. In the middle of it all there is a large, beautifully painted sign on a wall: 'Makululu belongs to Jesus'. Passing through the poverty, the dirt, the foul water, the cynic in me is tempted to say 'and he's welcome to it', but I know what the sign is getting at – a desperate people reaching out, a people forgotten or ignored by the better-off of their fellow citizens.

It's from Makululu that we draw most of our children. They come to us for education. They come to us for healthcare. They come to us for clothes. Most of all they come to us for food. Getting a place with us must be akin to winning the Lotto for these children who have nothing. There was no Lotto in Edmund Rice's time but the young people who found their way into Mount Sion from the slums of Waterford had surely struck it lucky. It is no doubt similar for the children of Makululu today. As we travel around Kabwe during the year doing home visits, dropping food and clothes to needy families and bringing the sick and the dying to hospital and hospice, we keep an eye out for the most needy cases and we add names to 'the list', i.e. the list of prospective pupils for the next Sables Nua enrolment.[2] By the time January comes around we usually have a fairly long list of names of very needy kids from Makululu and the other smaller but equally bad compounds. We post a sign on the gate: *'Takuli inchende'* ('This school is full – there are no more vacancies'), but it doesn't matter as still they come. It would break your heart.

'God our Father, please let my children be taken into this school'

At 5 a.m. on a fateful Wednesday in January I get a call from one of the guards: 'They are at the gate again. What will I do?' The 'they' he is referring to is the crowd of children and parents, grandparents or guardians who have gathered at our gate every morning since school re-opened. This particular morning the crowd is bigger than ever and the poor guard is worried that the scene might turn nasty. 'I'll be right there,' I say, 'and I'll talk to them. Tell them I'm coming'. By the time I get there the crowd, an orderly crowd in fairness, has swollen to quite a sizeable number, with children and adults pressed in a dense cordon around the gate. We'll have to do something, I think, and I ask them if they could clear a way for our staff and pupils to enter, and that once school had started I'd come to talk to them. That seems to go down well and we get over the first hurdle: getting the school up and running. When breakfast is finished and the classes have started, it's time to bite the bullet. There is a crowd of several hundred outside now – desperate people literally begging for a place in our school for one or more of their children. What do we do? We have only eight available spaces having already picked up children on the streets and on our travels around the compounds. I try to talk to the parents and guardians but there is just a babble of noise with people screaming out their difficulties and problems and pushing their children to the front of the queue, shouting 'Take my child! Take my child!' as another obviously malnourished, poorly dressed child is thrust towards me. People are on their knees begging, imploring, pleading ... and praying. 'God our Father, please let my children be taken into this school ...' is one prayer I hear over and over again. I wish that everybody around the world could hear them. I decide that we would have to talk to the children without the adults around and so we take all the children into the school, leaving their parents outside.

Like the Pied Piper of Hamelin of old, I lead a line of children, all ages and sizes, from the gate to the dining hall and get them to sit down. There are one hundred and twenty-seven children – I counted them – and we have space for fewer than ten. I look at them seated in front of me and what I see looking back is a sea of upturned, expectant faces – many malnourished, many dressed in rags, some obviously sick and all desperate to go to *'iskulu'* (school).

How can I do this, I think, playing God, picking out some children over others? This wasn't in the job description (actually there wasn't a job description!). God, you can have your job back! Who am I to choose between children, to decide who will get an education and who will never darken the door of a school? Who am I to decide who will be well-fed for the next ten or twelve years or who will live on scraps, who will be decently dressed or who will wear rags, who will have good healthcare or who will just struggle on? I can't do it, but I have to do it. I'll just pick; no scientific or educational criteria. Just get on with it, God help me, and get it over with – and do it now.

It's not a case of choosing who lives or who dies but it's not far off it. So I pick out some from the many, including a tiny little girl called Joy who looks like she'd break if you hugged her. My eye was drawn to another little girl named Martha who had a tuft of grey hair (a sign of severe malnutrition) and who somehow has great English. A scrawny boy with huge pleading eyes who stares straight through me, daring me to say 'no' to him perhaps; a girl who got dressed up in her finest to come beg for a chance of a decent future (her finest is a 'Snow White' dress, obviously discarded by a child in the so-called developed world, but this castaway party outfit is her best, probably only dress); and a boy with special needs get the nod. On we go until the maximum of eight becomes twenty and I separate this twenty from the others. No justification for the choice is possible. There is no logic and it might just as well have been a lottery; twenty to one side of me, one hundred and seven to the other side. Then I have to say the word to the children not 'selected', which I had been dreading. There is no way to soften the blow, for them or me. There is no carrot I can offer them nor hope I can hold out for them. *'Takuli inchende'* (in fact we're over-full). So it's a case of: *'Kabiyeni'* – 'you (plural), go away'. Simple as that, and they do. I'm close to tears as they acceptingly stand up and shuffle out the door, just another kick to them in their short, disadvantaged lives, as I watch them make their way to the gate and back to the margins. For a few minutes, they had hope, and now I've taken that hope away. I want to call them back and say 'F – – – it! We'll fit you in somehow. We'll find a way', but I know I can't, and I don't, and they all file out. All except one that is; one little lad, thinking I'm not looking, sees his chance and darts around the back of the kitchen and slips into the group of the chosen ones. Of course I pretend not to see him. God loves a trier, and I am playing God after all.

Makululu isn't the only place we find our children. We often pick them up, sometimes literally, on the streets. Hungry Lion is the main fast food joint in town. As it's next to the bus station it is one busy part of town. Hence it's a magnet for the street children. Whenever we have a runaway, we head for Hungry Lion and more often than not that's where we'll find our waifs and strays. About once a week we just wander there after dark to see if there are any new children on the street who we could maybe entice to Sables Nua, away from the streets. But the streets are an attractive place for many –

begging or stealing yields money, and money empowers; alcohol, glue and other drugs can relieve the pain, for a while anyway. I suppose it's the same the world over. I suppose it's always been the same. It was at Hungry Lion that we found Anthony.

Anthony – a child with impossible dreams

Anthony is, he thinks, fourteen years old and in grade four. He's quite old for that class but it's not uncommon here to have children with a huge variety of ages in the same class. Children come to school when they can but sometimes they may be needed at home for a few years to look after younger children, or may be required to go find some 'piecework' somewhere and only get to go to school when the parents or guardians can spare them.

'I am fourteen years old', he says, 'and I stay in Kamashanga.' Kamashanga is the third of the major compounds in Kabwe, after Makululu and Katondo. We draw around 70 per cent of our pupils from Makululu, maybe 15 per cent from Katondo, 10 per cent from Kamishanga and 5 per cent from miscellaneous parts of town. Kamashanga is about 7 km from Sables Nua, whereas the other compounds are closer. It's quite a walk, twice a day, to get to school. 'I have three brothers and three sisters and we stay in our home together with our mother and father,' Anthony informs. This, in itself, is unusual in the Sables' scheme of things as not too many of our children would have both parents alive or living with them. We have many 'double orphans', i.e. both parents dead, and very many 'single orphans', i.e. one parent dead. 'I am the second born,' he continues, 'My sister Maureen is the first born; the others are younger. Junior is the last born. I am the only child who goes to school. Our home has two rooms. My father is very sick and he stays in the home always. My mother is sick too but not as sick as my father.' Reading between the lines, it would seem that both parents are very ill, and those familiar with Zambia will know what that means – HIV/AIDS. He then explained his situation and what he did during the school holidays:

> My mother fell ill and she had to present to general hospital. There was no food in our home so my father said that since I was the first-born son I would have to get money for food. Every day I would rise early and walk to town. Then I would ask [beg] for money at the bus station. Some people would give me money but some would not. Some days I might get 10 Kwacha, some days even 15 Kwacha; one day I had 20 Kwacha. I would travel to my home when night was coming.

Ten Kwacha is a tiny sum of money – enough to buy a few tomatoes and 'leaves' to make a relish for supper. A tough life for a child, no matter how streetwise, and a big responsibility on young shoulders.

As a 'day pupil' on the street, Anthony got a hard time from some of the permanent residents of the streets who don't fancy casual beggars muscling in on their turf. 'I had to fight sometimes,' he says. 'The older ones wanted to take my money. Some others who had been in Sables were my friends so I was OK'. Like life in general, there is a hierarchy on the streets and some of the 'big bwanas' are former pupils of ours who have 'done a runner'. On his way home Anthony would buy relish and his sister would cook it. He would feed his father first and then the rest would eat. Then they would all go to sleep. When school began again his father said that he must go to school to be educated. His younger sister has now been sent out to get money for the family. How she 'earns' this is not through begging. She is not strong enough to stand up to boys who have that activity already sorted. There is only one way in which this young girl can get money to feed her family. She has no choice.

Anthony is a very well-spoken, pleasant and well-mannered young person. He plays for the school soccer team and has taken up judo and shows talent at that sport. He expresses an interest in becoming a doctor as he says that he wants to help others. He has no chance of realising this dream. As someone who has come to school as a late starter, he is highly unlikely to get to grade twelve and even if by some miracle he gets that far he will never spend a single day in college. He simply cannot afford the fees. Everything is stacked against him. The best we can hope for is that he will get a decent basic education here with us, including basic literacy and numeracy, and perhaps leave Sables Nua with a grade seven certificate, and maybe, just maybe, he might pick up some sort of a job. In the meantime, all we can do is see that Anthony is well fed, well clothed, well taken care of and very happy in Sables Nua. That, I suppose, is not a bad objective.

In the Western world, we surround ourselves with wealth and material possessions; we seek power and prestige and privileges; we chase happiness in trappings of wealth. In Kabwe, our children seek only basic food, clothing, shelter and education – real wealth. Many people in this world – too many – are ignorant or even indifferent to the pain and suffering of God's forgotten children, of people like Anthony. Pope Benedict XVI reminds and challenges us:

> We must do whatever we can to reduce suffering: to avoid as far as possible the suffering of the innocent; to soothe pain; to give assistance in overcoming

mental suffering. These are obligations both in justice and in love, and they are included among the fundamental requirements of the Christian life and every truly human life.[3]

We are what we are, but we don't have to stay that way and we don't have to allow the children of Kabwe to stay as they are either.

Reflection
- *Pádraig Ó Fainín was almost overwhelmed by the crowds at the gates of the school who were begged him to pick their children to be admitted. He wanted to run away. Yet he didn't. He could not do everything and choose everyone. So, he did everything that was in his power and changed the lives of some. Often we use the sheer scale and enormity of poverty and injustice as an excuse to turn our eyes away and do nothing.*
- *Have we the courage and compassion of Pádraig to do whatever we can, with whatever we have, wherever we are? Like those who passed by in the parable of the Good Samaritan, do we leave it to others to help those in need?*
- *Do we see those who are suffering as a political problem to be solved by politicians and government agencies or do we see them as our brothers and sisters in need of our help?*

Endnotes

1. In Zambia a 'compound' denotes a slum or shanty town.
2. Sables Nua is the name of the mission centre Pádraig has spent the past almost two decades supporting and developing.
3. Pope Benedict XVI, *Spe Salvi*, 36.

WALKING THROUGH WALLS: FR GERRY REYNOLDS' WITNESS AGAINST A DIVIDED CHRISTIANITY

Gladys Ganiel

It was 1983 when Redemptorist Fr Gerry Reynolds (1935–2015), like Blessed Edmund Rice before him, had his 'looking out the window' moment. He had just arrived in Clonard Monastery in Belfast, Northern Ireland. The Troubles (1968–98), which would claim more than 3,500 lives and injure and traumatise thousands more, were raging. Brother Hugh Murray took Gerry to a window on the third floor of the monastery. It had a panoramic view over the imposing 'peace wall' that separated the Catholic Falls area from the Protestant Shankill Road. Hugh had grown up in the gritty streets around Clonard. Now eighty years old, he had spent much of his ministry abroad and in other parts of Ireland. He told Gerry: 'They are all the same people – for generations the same factory hooters ruled their lives, calling them to the mills. They were all exploited and their differences were exaggerated to keep them divided. Neither group got a fair share of the wealth they created.'[1]

Gerry was moved by Hugh's compassion for *all* the people of the Shankill and the Falls, not just those on their 'side' of the peace wall. This 'looking out the window' moment confirmed Gerry's commitment to Christian unity. Over more than two decades of ministry in the Republic of Ireland, he had kindled a personal enthusiasm for ecumenism. But despite the island's troubled religious history, Protestants had become such a small minority in the Republic that the quest for Christian unity seemed inconsequential to most people. Not so in Northern Ireland. Even though the Troubles were not a holy war, divisions between Catholics and Protestants still mattered. Residential areas, schools and social networks were segregated along religious lines. Preachers like the fundamentalist Rev Ian Paisley of the Free Presbyterian Church were using religion to stoke fear and division. Paisley and his followers even organised noisy protests against ecumenical events like services during the Week of Prayer for Christian Unity. For Gerry, it was simple: 'A divided Church has little or nothing to offer towards leading a divided people into the way of peace. In the Northern Ireland conflict, divided Churches have cost lives.'[2]

I am an academic sociologist of religion, specializing in the role of religion in conflict and reconciliation. I also am Gerry's biographer.[3] I wanted to write the story of his life because I recognised that he, along with his Redemptorist colleague Fr Alec Reid, had played a decisive role in the Northern Ireland peace process. I also recognised that Gerry was an ecumenical pioneer. I believed that his innovative initiatives towards Christian unity could enrich the Church world-wide. As an American-born Protestant married to a Northern Irish Catholic, living in Northern Ireland, I see introducing Gerry's legacy to others as part of living out my own vocation.

In Edmund's day, Christian unity would have seemed implausible, if it even crossed people's minds. During his early life, Catholics in Ireland were subjected to Penal Laws, which ensured the privilege of a Protestant ruling class. Yet, as one biographer of Edmund reminds us, he had Quaker and Presbyterian friends who assisted him, contributing resources to his missions and helping convince the government to allow him to keep his schools open. If 'Edmund Rice was ahead of his time in his dealings with non-Catholics', at least in matters of practical cooperation,[4] Gerry also was ahead of his time in the ways he (literally) walked through walls to promote peace and Christian unity in his witness as a priest, especially through his role in the peace process, his creation of Unity Pilgrims and his work towards shared Eucharist.

The peace process
I have described Gerry as 'walking through walls', but one of his main contributions took place behind the walls of Clonard Monastery and in other discreet locations. Along with Fr Alec Reid, he helped facilitate secret peace talks among key political and religious leaders.[5] Alec had been in Clonard before the Troubles began and had developed a relationship with Sinn Féin politician Gerry Adams. Adams was regarded as a leader of the Irish Republican Army (IRA), although he has always denied belonging to the organisation. Sinn Féin and the IRA represented a republican perspective within the wider Catholic-nationalist-republican (CNR) community. Adams convinced Alec to broker secret talks between himself and the leader of the nationalist Social Democratic and Labour Party (SDLP), John Hume. At considerable risk, Hume agreed after receiving the invitation from Alec. Over time, Alec also facilitated communications between Sinn Féin, the IRA, and the British and Irish governments. Gerry attended some secret meetings with Alec, especially during the intense period leading up to the 1993 Downing Street Declaration and 1994 IRA ceasefire. Gerry also provided moral support

for Alec's demanding and emotionally exhausting work, praying with him and encouraging him.

Both Gerry and Alec believed violence would continue unless those who were engaged in it entered dialogue with others, a perspective captured in some of the first words Alec spoke to Gerry after he arrived in Clonard: 'The only way to change things, is through dialogue which makes room for the Holy Spirit to work in human history.'[6] They were convinced Sinn Féin and the IRA needed to encounter people and perspectives from the Protestant-unionist-loyalist (PUL) community. They also knew that no unionist politicians would risk meeting people from the IRA, even in secret, due to the taboo about 'talking with terrorists'. So they asked their Protestant clergy friends to attend secret talks with Sinn Féin and the IRA, in order to introduce all those involved to different perspectives. These talks began in 1990 and continued for fifteen years. They were so sensitive that many of the Protestant clergy who participated have still not revealed their involvement. Various Sinn Féin politicians have attested to the value of the talks;[7] Gerry himself said, 'The fruit of it was it helped human relationships. It helped to create a human understanding of people who were ideologically in very different places.'[8]

At the same time, Gerry contributed to the peace process through a passionate, public ecumenical ministry. Along with Presbyterian Rev. Ken Newell, he was central to the development of the Clonard–Fitzroy Presbyterian Fellowship. Clonard–Fitzroy provided safe, private spaces for people to encounter each other on a human and spiritual level. It also organised important public events such as a 1986 discussion between the Presbyterian moderator and a Catholic bishop – which drew fierce protests from Free Presbyterians – and civic dialogues with politicians after the 1994 ceasefire, among many others over the decades. Clonard–Fitzroy was awarded the 1999 Pax Christi International Peace Prize for its exemplary grassroots peacebuilding.

Gerry was also deeply involved with Cornerstone, an ecumenical residential community located along the Falls–Shankill peace wall. Cornerstone developed from a Bible study group that had met in Clonard from the early 1980s. It modelled an alternative way of living together in the midst of sectarian violence, rooted in daily, structured prayers for peace. It later partnered with secular and religious groups in social development projects. Gerry was a non-resident member of Cornerstone, so he regularly journeyed from Clonard to join the community for prayers and to participate in its projects. He forged a strong friendship with Methodist Rev. Sam Burch, who led Cornerstone for many years. In 1986, after the IRA murder of an Ulster Defence Regiment sergeant in the Shankill, Gerry yearned to visit the grieving family. As a Catholic priest, this would have been unprecedented and likely impossible. But he convinced Sam to go with him. The visit was emotional but cathartic. Gerry returned to the family on other occasions, accompanied at least once by four religious sisters. In the years that followed, Gerry and Sam visited more than fifty families, most within one mile of either side of the peace wall. Other Cornerstone members took part in this ministry, visiting as pairs of Catholics and Protestants. In this way, Gerry and his friends comforted the grieving and the traumatised. It also is possible that their compassionate witness helped dampen angry emotions and the desire for revenge. I cannot quantify how much Gerry and his friends helped those they encountered or how far the ripple effect of their witness extended in the wider community but I am confident enough to conclude that their work was 'immeasurable' in the sense of bringing something of infinite value to the peace process.

Unity Pilgrims

On Remembrance Sunday 1994, Gerry felt prompted in his spirit to join a Protestant congregation for worship. In Northern Ireland, Remembrance Sunday is a major occasion in most Protestant churches, with services honouring those killed during the Troubles alongside those who died in the world wars. Catholic churches do not mark the day. Gerry recalled: 'I decided, on a sudden impulse, to go on my own from Clonard Monastery to worship with a congregation of the Church in the Shankill. I cannot remember now which one it was. It just seemed right to me that I should worship together with them on that special Sunday.'[9] Over the coming weeks, Gerry continued walking through the peace wall to join other Protestant congregations for worship. He soon invited Catholic members of Cornerstone to accompany him. This marked the small beginnings of an initiative that still operates out of Clonard: the Unity Pilgrims.

The Unity Pilgrims were warmly received by the Protestant congregations. This was due in part to the patient witness of Gerry and Cornerstone over the previous decade. They were also respectful about how they went about their visits, arranging the date beforehand with the minister. They emphasised that they came in friendship to worship – not to proselytise. They did not sit together as a group but rather spread out among the congregation, all the better to strike up conversation afterwards. Their preparation for the visits included meeting on Thursday evenings in a convent for an hour of prayer, and a further thirty minutes of prayer before departing on the Sunday morning. Gerry explained:

> Before setting out we always take a while to focus ourselves in Jesus' prayer: 'Father, may they all be one.' We see our visits as planting new seeds of

friendship and prayer between the congregations of the Church in the Shankill and those in the Falls and as a communal response to Jesus' command to 'Love one another as I have loved you'.[10]

Gerry dreamed that one day there would be Unity Pilgrims in every parish in the world, small but dedicated bands who would go out to pray and worship alongside Christians of other traditions. In this way, Gerry believed that Unity Pilgrims would bear witness to the reality, rather than simply the aspiration, of Christian unity. In 2010 he helped produce a study guide, *Catholic Unity Pilgrims: Parishioners Enhancing Faith and Church*, which was commended by the local bishop. Its purpose was to encourage Catholic parishes to create their own Unity Pilgrims. Clonard has never attempted to quantify how many groups resulted from this publication. I am aware of a few – including at least one group of Presbyterian Unity Pilgrims – but my sense is that their numbers were small and most of the groups have ceased to exist. Clonard's own Unity Pilgrims are an ageing and diminishing group. Even so, I see the Unity Pilgrims as one of Gerry's most creative and powerful initiatives – deceptively simple in the way it encourages people to simply be together in a spirit of friendship. The Unity Pilgrims' basic commitment to walk through walls is one that can be replicated across the 'dividing walls' that are present in every society, whether of religion, race, ethnicity, class, gender, etc.

Shared Eucharist

Gerry shed many tears over canon law's prohibition on shared Eucharist. In groups like Clonard–Fitzroy and Cornerstone, where people had developed strong spiritual bonds, the desire to partake together in this central Christian rite seemed natural. At times Gerry expressed frustration, as in 1988:

> Members of the Catholic Church, except in very exceptional circumstances, are not allowed to welcome members of the Protestant Churches to share in sacramental communion with them. That is the law our legislators have made for us. But one wonders about a process of law making in which the *'nepioi'* [little children] in no way participate.
>
> Jesus said 'Unless you become as little children you shall not enter the kingdom of heaven' (Mt 18:3). Is there not an urgent call of the Spirit to the whole Church to reconsider, in humble childlike openness to Him, our rules about intercommunion – rules which, at the sacramental memorial of Our Lord's Passion, institutionalize the scandal of our failure to witness as one family to His all-embracing, reconciling gift of love?[11]

Over the course of his life, Gerry received communion in Protestant settings; at other times, he distributed to Protestants.[12] These were small, private occasions. Aware that there are exceptions to the prohibition on shared Eucharist in canon law, Gerry always provided his reasons for doing so in his private diaries, describing each occasion and his rationale.

Gerry believed that the unity of Christians was already a reality, so he longed for that to be reflected in full communion at the Lord's table. His faith in the 'invisible' unity of all Christians was buttressed by the witness of Fr Paul Couturier (1881–1953), a French priest who helped establish the Week of Prayer for Christian Unity. Gerry often repeated the phrase Couturier had printed on his first prayer card for Christian Unity, produced in 1934: 'the walls of separation do not reach to heaven'. This also was the motto of a bi-weekly column

Gerry wrote in the *Irish News*, a secular newspaper, between 1987 and 1989. He used the penname 'Couturier'.

Despite my research, I cannot pronounce with certainty Gerry's position on shared Eucharist; in fact, it seems he had various positions over the course of his life. When he chose to partake, his convictions were guided by the context – and what he interpreted as the leading of the Holy Spirit.

In 2010, Gerry and his long-time friend Methodist Rev. Dennis Cooke helped start an initiative called 'In Joyful Hope: A New Step in Eucharistic Fellowship'. Like the Unity Pilgrims, In Joyful Hope was a simple, public witness. It involved Gerry and his friends organising regular services of Communion at churches from different denominations. The group's guidelines, which were affirmed by the local bishop, stated that 'Eucharistic discipline of the Roman Catholic Church would be observed in the group's public events.' Among the group's 'reasons for doing this' were 'to anticipate in so far as we can the common Holy Communion/Eucharist we yearn for'.[13] So in this initiative, Gerry publicly observed Eucharistic discipline in the hope of putting shared Eucharist back on the agenda.

Indeed, it seems shared Eucharist has slipped off the ecumenical agenda across the world. And it could be tempting to view Gerry's preoccupation with it as a distraction from his peacebuilding ministry. But Gerry did not separate peacebuilding from shared Eucharist; for him, they were inextricably bound together. Gerry's emphasis on shared Eucharist reminds us that witnessing against a divided Christianity is as much a spiritual battle as one rooted in the practical work of grassroots peacebuilding.

Walking through walls

If Gerry could look out the window from the third floor of Clonard today, he would still see that imposing peace wall.

It is a stark reminder that his journey is unfinished. Gerry died in the hope that others would continue walking through walls, until everyone began to believe that they could live better together without them.

I was privileged to write Gerry's biography and I want to continue sharing his story. I am working in partnership with Clonard and a facilitator, Dave Thompson, to create study resources based around Gerry's life for Clonard's youth and reconciliation ministries. I hope those who learn about Gerry will be inspired to respond to Northern Ireland's continuing divisions in creative ways. Maybe some will become Unity Pilgrims; perhaps others will create entirely new initiatives. I also am involved with Belfast's annual 4 Corners Festival, founded in 2013 by Fr Martin Magill and Presbyterian Rev. Steve Stockman.[14] Belfast is still geographically divided on religious lines, so 4 Corners stages events in these segregated 'corners', encouraging people to go to areas they would not enter in their everyday lives. Using the creative arts, prayer and public dialogue, it offers Christian perspectives on Belfast's unfinished journey towards peace and Christian unity. Gerry attended some 4 Corners events before his death; I am confident he approved of how it encourages people to literally walk through Belfast's walls.

But beyond Belfast, there are windows all over the world that look out over bitterly divided societies. Gerry's witness against a divided Christianity teaches us to respond to divisions not only with compassionate, practical action, but also with a spirituality rooted in the Eucharist, in that way embodying the unity that has already been achieved for all Christians, through Christ.

Reflection
- Gladys Ganiel sees Fr Gerry Reynolds as a prophetic voice in a society that is often defined in terms of its separation, division and mutual distrust. When Fr Gerry looked out the window of his monastery he did not see 'peace lines' and 'the other'; rather, he saw his fellow brothers and sisters and reached out to them as such. Gladys urges us to see difference not as a challenge or a problem to be overcome but as a rich gift to be embraced and cherished.
- In our lives, do we view people of different religious or political beliefs as 'others' or as outsiders?
- Do we use our own beliefs and practices as markers of inclusion and exclusion?
- Do we use the gospel and the Christian message to reach out to others in unity or to build walls to exclude?

Endnotes

1. Quoted in Ronald Wells, *Friendship Towards Peace: The Journey of Ken Newell and Gerry Reynolds*, Dublin: Columba, 2004, p. 49.
2. Quoted in Gladys Ganiel, *Unity Pilgrim: The Life of Fr Gerry Reynolds CSsR*, Dundalk: Redemptorist Communications, 2019, p. 87.
3. Ibid.
4. James A. Houlihan, *Overcoming Evil with Good: The Edmund Rice Story*, New Rochelle, NY: Iona College, 1997, p. 141.
5. Martin McKeever, *One Man, One God: The Peace Ministry of Fr Alec Reid CSsR*, Dublin: Redemptorist Communications, 2017.
6. Quoted in Ganiel, *Unity Pilgrim*, p. 85.
7. John D. Brewer, Gareth I. Higgins and Francis Teeney, *Religion, Civil Society and Peace in Northern Ireland*, Oxford: Oxford University Press, 2011, p. 63–4.
8. Quoted in Ganiel, *Unity Pilgrim*, p. 171.
9. Quoted in Ronald Wells, *Hope and Reconciliation in Northern Ireland*, Dublin: Liffey Press, 2010, p. 135–6.

10 Ibid., p. 136–7.
11 Quoted in Ganiel, *Unity Pilgrim*, p. 159.
12 Ibid., p. 240.
13 Ibid., p. 238.
14 See https://4cornersfestival.com/.

A PILGRIMAGE FOR JUSTICE AND PEACE[1]

Lesley O'Connor

Serendipity

It was easy to notice while sharing breakfast in Dromantine Retreat Centre in Newry, County Down, in March 2015, that these women were upset. Israeli women of Jewish and Muslim faiths, in Ireland to participate in a leadership programme. News of Benjamin Netanyahu's re-election had just been announced, and their hope for a peaceful future seemed to evaporate. I wondered what was happening in their broken country, the place that I knew as the Holy Land. I immediately decided that I wanted to go there, not on a tourist pilgrimage to the holy places that I knew by faith; I wanted to learn more about the lives of the people who struggled daily with the sad reality expressed by these women who still found a way to make a stand for peace.

Edmund Ignatius Rice is said to have found his call to action by following the request of Waterford woman Mary Power to look outside his window. My observation at a breakfast table in Northern Ireland was perhaps my window moment. I was drawn to look for a way to learn more, to be of service and to deal with my judgements and suppositions about life in Israel and Palestine.

I returned to Waterford and continued on with my work as a service manager with Brothers of Charity Services in Waterford. My job was my vocation – did I need another? A few days later, as I rounded Reginald Tower and drove up the Quay in Waterford, I was brought back to that window. Waterford Quay, so well known to Edmund Ignatius Rice and the scene of his work to educate the poor. In hindsight, it was serendipitous that it was there I was called to listen and to see a way to be of service.

As I drove on that beautiful sunny morning I listened to a woman called Jenny being interviewed by broadcaster Marian Finucane about her time as a human rights observer on the West Bank. I was transfixed. Over and over in my mind I repeated, 'I could do that'. I parked the car, rummaged for pen and paper and scribbled out the initials EAPPI (The Ecumenical Accompaniment Programme in Palestine and Israel). With a little effort on Google I was in contact with the office of the programme in the Quaker Headquarters in London. They put me in contact with Jenny Derbyshire, the woman I heard on the radio. She was a tremendous encouragement and refused to allow me to be dissuaded despite only five from Ireland being chosen to participate in the programme each year. My application was successful and in August 2017 I flew to Tel Aviv to begin my three-month pilgrimage for justice and peace with the World Council of Churches' Ecumenical Accompaniment Programme.[2]

Israel–Palestine peace issues
The history of the state of Israel and occupied Palestine is sad and complex. November 2017 marked the centenary of the Balfour Declaration when the British recognised that the Jewish people had a right to return to their homeland.[3] The Balfour Declaration also declared in the same sixty-seven-

word sentence: 'it being clearly understood that nothing shall be done which may prejudice the civil and religious rights of existing non-Jewish communities in Palestine'. The interpretation and practise of this right of Jewish people to return to a homeland has impacted on the lives of the Palestinian people who were already living there. Many have suffered displacement and now live in refugee camps. The Israeli military occupation of the West Bank commenced in 1967 and continues to this day, causing restrictions and loss of human rights in the lives of the Palestinian people.

Being present in the West Bank for the centenary commemorations in November 2017 made it clear to me that many of the Palestinian people view the Balfour Declaration as the defining cause of the current conflict. On the day of the centenary I attended an academic event in the National Palestinian Theatre in East Jerusalem at which scholars discussed the Balfour Declaration from many perspectives. Later I attended a service of penance in St George's Anglican Cathedral, Jerusalem, which remains in my memory for two reasons. First, that it was there I was reunited with Jenny, the woman I heard on the radio. She was there participating in Amos Trust action: 'Just Walk to Jerusalem'.[4] The second reason this event remains in memory is symptomatic of life under occupation. The magnificent choir from Bethlehem, coming to sing at the cathedral, was held up at a checkpoint. The congregation waited patiently until the choir finally got through the checkpoint and arrived to delight us with their songs of peace.

Background to World Council of Churches peacebuilding programme
In 2002 the Christian churches in Jerusalem made a plea to the World Council of Churches to send observers to

experience life under occupation and to monitor the human rights injustices that were taking place in Jerusalem and the West Bank in contravention of international law.[5] The World Council of Churches responded by setting up the Ecumenical Accompaniment Programme in Palestine and Israel.[6] The vision of the programme is to see an end to the occupation and to secure a just peace for all Israeli and Palestinian people. The mission of the programme is to witness life under occupation, to engage with Palestinian and Israeli peacemakers and to encourage international communities' involvement in the conflict by urging action. Ecumenical accompaniers representing twenty-three countries currently participate in the programme. Placements have been developed on request from communities who appreciate an international presence. When I was there the placements were located in seven communities in the West Bank – Bethlehem, Jerusalem, Tulkarem, Yanoun, Jericho, Hebron and South Hebron Hills.

Pilgrim stories
'Part of the journey entails meeting other pilgrims along the way and being shaped by their stories.'[7] In deciding to make a pilgrimage we are called to walk with other people. The role of an ecumenical accompanier is about being an observer and a listener. In observing breaches of human rights that contravene international humanitarian law, we listen to, and bear witness to, the stories of those who have been mistreated. We also listen to, and bear witness to, those who strive to be peacemakers, many of them Israeli Jewish citizens. Each day, for three months, I encountered people and their stories. In this way, I, the accompanier, was also accompanied and transformed by those who welcomed me to share their lives. My mission in South Hebron Hills was to give 'protective presence' when requested using 'principled

impartiality'.[8] As an ecumenical accompanier I did not take sides in the conflict, I stood as an impartial observer but I was not impartial with regards to breaches in international humanitarian law.

The impact of the occupation on the communities of South Hebron Hills and the West Bank is evident in the daily lives of all who live there. Palestinian people live lives of restriction in terms of movement to school and work. Children and adults have to queue to pass through checkpoints sometimes for hours each day in order to access education or employment. The right to a new home is practically non-existent due to the arbitrary planning laws. House demolitions take place without any concern for people's needs or rights.

The Israeli people also suffer. Much of their economy is channelled towards security. Young adults endure compulsory military service. I came to know this impact over and over again as I met Jewish mothers, fathers and grandparents. What must it feel like for the Jewish mother of a newborn knowing that her child will, as a teenager, be put into uniform and heavily armed?

As I travelled I met people who lived their spirituality in the face of seemingly insurmountable difficulties. Their lives shone through as a beacon of hope for the future. The following is my witness to three women's stories.

The grandmother in the firing zone
It is a long drive to the Bedouin village of al Halaweh inside the Israeli-military dubbed 'Firing Zone 918'.[9] Much of the journey in this part of the West Bank is on dirt roads. Our driver appears uneasy. These roads are not good for his car, and without his car he has no livelihood. The Israeli military have a base less than one kilometre from al Halaweh; we do not want to meet them. As we pass two large cubes of mass

concrete our driver declares: 'We are now in the firing zone'. Despite his misgivings, he agreed to bring us to the Bedouin village when we received a request to visit families and compile a report after the military demolished two houses. When we arrive, he directs us to the brow of a sand dune overlooking the village.

Here we meet Hiba, whose family has withstood one of the demolitions. She greets us and welcomes us to take photographs. She cradles her newborn granddaughter. Baby Dahlia is dressed in beautiful fabric and smiling up at her grandmother. 'The bulldozers arrived at 9 a.m.,' she explains. 'They gave us a half an hour to take out our belongings, but it was not long enough.' As she speaks my gaze rests on a child's blue bike still trapped in the debris of the family's two-roomed home. Hiba remains composed as she speaks. At her side stands her other granddaughter, Samar, a beautiful, smiling two-year-old wearing a 'Hello Kitty' top. Somehow Samar's grandmother manages to maintain family life, and this little girl remains smiling.

When I ask where she is living now Hiba says that the family of eight, comprising three adults and five young girls, have now moved into the caves adjacent to the demolition site. Scorpions and snakes found in these caves are a cause of concern as medical treatment is not accessible for those who suffer bites. Life in the military firing zone is unpredictable and chaotic yet Hiba and her family continue their daily life as best they can, creating a home despite the demolitions. Life goes on with the support of a tight-knit community where neighbours support each other through each tragedy.

As we continue to gather information for our report, we learn that the village elders had been working with a legal team who advise on responses to human rights breaches that the Bedouin people suffer. It turns out Hiba's home and the other dwelling that was demolished on that day had been covered by a legal injunction not to demolish. All that appears capricious now. On the long drive back, I reflect on the immensity of it all. Not once did I hear a word of hate or even despair. I think of the lives of little Samar and her baby sister Dahlia. I wonder at the grace and determination of the Bedouin people of al Halaweh who continue to welcome the stranger and love their neighbours in the face of constant adversity.

The destruction or demolition of private and public property by the Occupying Power is prohibited under Articles 53 and 147 of the Fourth Geneva Convention and under Article 23 of the 1907 Hague Regulations, unless absolutely necessary for military operations.

The woman at the wall

Curious about a meeting for prayer that I have heard occurs every Friday at the separation wall, I travel up through Hebron and arrive in Bethlehem just in time to find out where to join the prayer group.[10] It is almost six o'clock as I approach the group of about fifteen men and women, mostly Christian religious internationals, recognisable by their habits, gathering at the separation wall. 'Thank you for coming. Where are you from?' When I respond 'Ireland', a welcoming cheer rings out and the Friday prayer at the wall commences.

When Israel began building the twenty-foot-high separation wall in Bethlehem in 2003, Clemence, a farmer, was cut off from her land and neighbours. She pondered about what she could do. 'I realised that I could pray. So, each Friday, I pray with those who come and share with me. I pray for those who have lost their land because of the occupation. I pray for the soldiers who work here at the separation wall. What else can I do?'

The group walks in procession along the part of the separation wall that divides Clemence's land. A rosary is shared, each decade in a different language, representing the pilgrims who gather each Friday to accompany Clemence. As we come to the end of our prayer, we gather in front of an icon of Mary that was written on the separation wall by the British icon writer Ian Knowles in 2010. The icon of *Our Lady of the Wall* is situated here as a symbol of faith, hope and love.[11] It is a non-violent sign to express the need to overcome the injustice that the separation wall imposes on landowners like Clemence. It is a prayer for peace. It is a prayer that one day the wall will go away. This is the mission of the Friday prayer at the wall. This simple prayer action has created for Clemence and her people a community of love, solidarity and goodwill in the face of adversity.

Gatekeepers

Our work as ecumenical accompaniers is enriched by witnessing the actions of Israeli human rights organisations. One such organisation is Machsom Watch.[12] Hanna Barak, its founder, met us one stifling hot day. Hanna, a tiny grandmother, sat serenely as we entered the room, took our seats, and looked for water to cool ourselves.

In 2001, when Israeli checkpoints began to impact on the right to movement in the lives of Palestinian people, a group of Israeli Jewish women felt compelled to take action. Machsom Watch was formed to assist Palestinian people with permit denial and occasions of hostility or delay experienced at checkpoints. A phone line is operated by Machsom Watch for those who experience illegal restrictions. People are given legal support to object to the Israeli authorities about the injustices that they are experiencing. Hanna explained that she is part of this movement because she is a good Israeli Jewish woman and she believes that what is happening at checkpoints is unjust and illegal. The work that Hanna and the other woman in Machsom Watch carry out is a lifeline for many Palestinians. It is also dangerous. Hanna has been abused and vilified many times and she has even been physically attacked. Hanna continues her work because she believes that Israel, as a modern democratic country, should not treat people with disrespect by impinging on their human rights. The presence of Machsom Watch at checkpoints serves to encourage Israeli security personnel to act with respect to the many thousands of Palestinians who have no choice but to pass through checkpoints to go to work, school or prayer.

As an accompanier, one of my most soul-destroying duties was to stand and watch men queue at a checkpoint in the dark of the night waiting patiently to be allowed to pass through to go to work on the buildings in Israel. Many of them are university graduates who need to work as labourers in order to support their families. Their days are consumed with getting through the checkpoints and hopefully picking up work on a piecemeal basis. Each time I stood at a checkpoint I observed men being denied entry. As they were rejected I asked why they had been denied. Some had been given a reason, others did not know why they had been denied. It was good to be able to offer those denied information about Machsom Watch. In a place where there seems to be no prospect for self-determination for Palestinians, Hanna and the women at Machsom Watch have created a possibility of expertise and care for calling out injustices and putting the goodness of their faith into action.

To enforce movement restrictions, Israel instituted a permit system that requires all Palestinian residents of the Occupied Territories to obtain a permit in order to enter Israel, including East Jerusalem, for any purpose whatsoever – including work, medical care and family visits.[13]

Basic core of goodness
During my journey, I met people who were making choices for justice and peace even when it appeared that they were oppressed and without choice. Again and again, I was touched by the basic core of goodness in people that compelled them to respond in their own unique way to seemingly impossible situations in their lives. Pope Francis has marked his pontificate by his ongoing urge to live the word of God: 'To follow Jesus, mere good works are not enough; we have to listen daily to his call. He, who alone knows us and who loves us fully, leads us to push out into the depth of life.'[14] As I walked the Holy Land, I met people who chose mercy and love instead of hatred and despair. Leaving her family rudderless is not an option for Hiba. When all seems lost, Clemence continues to pray for the neighbour she can no longer meet. Hanna chooses to be an agent of justice and peace and change because she is good Jewish woman.

One more window
In October 2019 I visited Kraków in Poland. Something urged me to come and stand in the Auschwitz and Birkenau camps as part of my pilgrimage. While there, I also visited Schindler's factory. Our guide was a tiny Jewish woman called Christina. At one stage she stopped at a window and explained to us that Oskar Schindler had looked out on the street and saw a woman crossing the road holding the hand of a little girl in a red coat. In that moment, he was immediately moved

to do something to save the children who were in danger of being removed to extermination camps. As I stood there listening to Oskar's story I remembered Edmund and how he had been urged by Mary Power to look out the window to find his calling.

Conclusion
For three months, I shared life with pilgrims in the land central to the tenets of the three largest monotheistic religions: Judaism, Christianity and Islam. As a contemplative, it was of no surprise that this ecumenical programme was the one to which I was drawn. It was an opportunity to reconsider my story, to connect with the biblical values of social justice in a parched landscape where people of all denominations suffer. Meeting people on a heart-to-heart basis went beyond the reasons for the conflict, beyond the labels of faith traditions, and brought me on a pilgrimage of love and respect for each pilgrim I met. Cistercian monk Thomas Keating puts it well:

> The great treasure that interreligious dialogue among the world religions could unlock is to enable people to get to know and love other religions and the people who practice them. The attitude of exclusivity must be laid to rest. God is too big to be contained in one religion.[15]

Reflection
- *Lesley recalled that it was on Waterford Quay, so familiar to Edmund, that she heard about the programme that inspired her call to service. Looking back, can you connect to a moment, an encounter or a place that changed your path?*
- *In the Middle East, is a ministry of 'protective presence' and 'principled impartiality' a worthwhile approach in your*

opinion? *The grandmother in the military firing zone had her house demolished. Would you have responded as she responded? The woman at the separation wall said she realised she could pray, if nothing else. What would you say to these women?*
- *Both Edmund Rice and Oskar Schindler looked out a window and took action. Is there a window that you are looking out today that might move you to action?*

Endnotes

1 Some names have been changed in this chapter for privacy reasons.
2 The World Council of Churches is a worldwide fellowship of churches seeking unity, a common witness and Christian service. See https://www.oikoumene.org/about-the-wcc.
3 The Balfour declaration was the first time the British government endorsed the establishment of 'a national home for the Jewish people' in Palestine. While many Israelis believe it was the foundation stone of modern Israel and the salvation of the Jews, many Palestinians regard it as a betrayal. See Jane Corbin, 'The Balfour Declaration: My Ancestor's Hand in History', *BBC News*, 31 October 2017. Available at http://www.bbc.com/news/world-middle-east-41763648; accessed 11 February 2020.
4 See https://www.amostrust.org/blog/just-walk-to-jerusalem-2017/.
5 See, for example, www.wcc-coe.org/wcc/what/international/advocacy.html.
6 On the Ecumenical Accompaniment Programme in Palestine and Israel (EAPPI), see https://eappi.org/en/about.
7 Emily Welty, *Beginning the Pilgrimage towards Justice*, 2013. Available at https://www.oikoumene.org/sites/default/files/Document/Beginning_the_pilgrimage-E_Welty.pdf; accessed on 20 May 2022.
8 'Protective Presence – Our presence makes the costs of human rights abuses more apparent to the perpetrators, persuades them to act differently, and deters attacks on civilians'; 'Principled Impartiality – We do not take sides in the conflict. We do not discriminate against anyone and stand faithfully with the poor, the oppressed, and the marginalized.' See EAPPI, 'Our Model'. Available at https://eappi.org/en/our-model; accessed 11 February 2020.

9   See EA Lesley, 'They knocked down the wrong house', *Eyewitness Blogs*, 6 November 2017. Available at https://web.archive.org/web/20180215030417/https://eyewitnessblogs.com/2017/11/06/they-knocked-down-the-wrong-house/; accessed 24 May 2022.

10 See EA Paul, 'Bethlehem: "That the wall will fall into a bridge"', *Eyewitness Blogs*, 5 February 2018. Available at https://web.archive.org/web/20180511161459/https://www.eyewitnessblogs.com/2018/02/05/bethelehem-that-the-wall-will-fall-into-a-bridge/; accessed 22 May 2022.

11 See http://sacredplaces.huji.ac.il/sites/our-lady-wall.

12 The Israeli Machsom Watch group engages in similar work to EAPPI, monitoring the treatment of Palestinian workers coming through daily checkpoints from the West Bank to work in Israel. See https://machsomwatch.org/en/content/bureaucracy-occupation.

13 See https://www.btselem.org/freedom_of_movement.

14 Pope Francis, quoted in Inés San Martín, 'Pope Francis says the Bible is a "love letter" from God', *Crux*, 26 January 2020. Available at https://cruxnow.com/vatican/2020/01/pope-francis-says-the-bible-is-a-love-letter-from-god/; accessed 25 May 2022.

15 Thomas Keating, *Consenting to God as God Is,* New York: Lantern Books, 2016, p. 5.

TERRA NULLIUS, AUSTRALIAN INDIGENOUS POLICY AND THE CHARISM OF EDMUND RICE

Darryl Cronin

Introduction

When Lieutenant James Cook dismissed the sovereignty of Indigenous people and claimed the east coast of the Australian continent for the British Crown in August 1770, Edmund Rice, the founder of the Christian Brothers in Ireland, along with other Irish Catholics, was living under the last vestiges of Penal Laws.[1] The Penal Laws, which originated in England and were imposed in Ireland in 1695, were a series of laws against religion, education, property and social activities in an effort to prevent not only the practice of the Catholic faith in England and Ireland but also dispossess Catholics of their civil rights, property rights and dignity.

Edmund Rice was a young boy when Lieutenant James Cook claimed the entire east coast of the Australian continent. Cook took possession of the continent on an island detached from the mainland, which he named 'Possession Island'. The Kaurareg people inhabited the island. His manner of claiming the continent set the scene for an ongoing relationship of disrespect with Indigenous people that is underpinned by erroneous assumptions and demeaning discourses. Such assumptions and discourses provided justification for the British to conclude that the entire continent was terra nullius ('nobody's land'), a convenient fiction used to legally justify British occupation of Indigenous land and to deny Indigenous rights. Cook and his colleague Joseph Banks perpetrated these assumptions and discourses through their dismissal of Indigenous polity and their view that Indigenous people were too uncivilised to have any form of society, property or sovereignty.

In 1788, when the British Crown began dispossessing Indigenous nations in Australia of their lands and extending British rule over their territories, Catholics in Ireland had endured dispossession, persecution, oppression and various restrictions for nearly a hundred years under the Penal Laws. The Penal Laws prevented the practice of the Catholic faith, dispossessed Catholics of their land and undermined their economic and political power. The laws alienated the Catholic population, weakened the Catholic Church and had an enduring impact on Irish society. However, by the late 1770s, some of the Penal Laws were repealed, paving the way for the political and social resurgence of the Catholic population and the revival of contemporary Irish Catholicism. From 1778 onwards the Penal Laws were dismantled, and, by the early nineteenth century, Catholics could be elected to parliament, hold public offices and vote.

The Rice family endured the impact of the Penal Laws. Edmund Rice attended a Catholic school, which was illegal under Penal Laws. In 1779 he began an apprenticeship at his uncle Michael Rice's business in Waterford. He eventually inherited the business through which he gained social and business prominence. He was a practising Catholic and very active in Catholic politics. After the sudden death of his wife in 1789, Rice sought spiritual solace in prayer and the Bible.

His priorities in life began to change as he saw the injustices stemming from the treatment of Catholics as second-class citizens. He undertook charity work with orphans, prisoners and the poor of Waterford. In 1800, when the British were in the throes of their invasion in Australia, Edmund Rice commenced his work in Ireland providing Catholic education to the poor. His work would play a vital role in rebuilding and empowering Irish society.

As Irish Catholics were gaining freedoms from the 1770s onwards, Indigenous Australians were being subjected to the yoke of colonialism. This chapter examines how Indigenous Australians have struggled against colonialism and especially how colonial assumptions and discourses have portrayed Indigenous people as inferior. The thinking behind these assumptions and discourses has dispossessed Indigenous people of their sovereignty, property rights, civil rights, and dignity. This thinking, which I call 'terra nullius thinking', has been influential in the relationship between Indigenous people and the Australian State. Australian society must move beyond such thinking and this is where the charism of Edmund Rice and the Irish Catholic resurgence is relevant. The charism of Edmund Rice is a special gift of power and influence that is applied for the benefit and good of others. Rice reached out to provide spiritual and material nourishment, educating the disadvantaged and dispossessed, thereby empowering Irish Catholic society as it emerged from the impacts of the Penal Laws. There is need for a similar compassion in Australia if the nation is to emerge from colonialism and create a relationship of respect and recognition with Indigenous people.

Understanding the past
The thinking that portrays Indigenous people as inferior and deficient emerged in Europe during the age of colonial

expansion and the acquisition of foreign territories. Indigenous people were portrayed as 'barbarians' and 'savages' to justify European claims to their territories. By the nineteenth century it was common to deny sovereignty and ownership of land to Indigenous peoples. This change produced the modern doctrine of terra nullius that was applied to the Australian continent.

Lieutenant James Cook and Joseph Banks wrote in their journals that the Australian continent was sparsely populated, that Aboriginal people had no houses nor had any settled form of habitation, had nothing of value and had no idea of trade, and did not cultivate the land. These views have been influential in propagating erroneous assumptions and discourses that Aboriginal people were culturally inferior, lacking property ownership, civilisation, law, government and sovereignty. This in turn provided the justification for the British to treat the Australian continent as terra nullius. Terra nullius lands were regarded as either wholly unoccupied or occupied by people who were considered too 'barbarous' or 'savage' to have legal, social and political systems worthy of recognition.

These false assumptions became part of the beliefs, policies and laws of the British colonies in Australia. Indigenous rights were considered non-existent, therefore terra nullius thinking became embedded in the constitutional, legal and policy framework of Australia. Furthermore, over the course of history, an intellectual framework that is resistant to recognising and respecting Indigenous people has become influential in Australia and has become part of the language, culture and practices of government and society. This framework influences how Indigenous people are perceived and treated and it has spawned an array of negative and demeaning views and opinions about Indigenous Australians.

The legal framework

According to British law, the Australian continent was unclaimed territory; therefore, Indigenous people were considered to have lost all rights, titles and interest in land in 1788. Several legal cases consistently articulated this view and they show how the courts used erroneous colonial assumptions about Indigenous people to deny Indigenous rights to land and sovereignty.

In the 1800s, court decisions judged Indigenous people as being too small in numbers, not having the strength to be considered a sovereign nation and that there was no land law or land tenure existing in Australia. The continent was regarded as unoccupied because Indigenous people were considered to have no settled laws. Between 1836 and 1992, courts in Australia largely accepted these false assumptions. In 1970 when Yolngu clans in Arnhem Land in the Northern Territory asserted their rights to their land and their customs, their claims were dismissed on the basis that the Crown had acquired sovereignty over Australia and therefore was the only source of all rights, title and interests in land. It was wrongly asserted that the Yolngu did not have a proprietary interest in land.

Australian courts continued to apply erroneous assumptions up until 1992, thereby dismissing the rights of Indigenous people on the basis they had no laws and land ownership and consequently no sovereignty. The courts also affirmed that the annexation of the east of Australia in 1770 and subsequent acts of colonisation were acts of State, which could not be challenged. The judicial view that the colony of New South Wales and the Australian continent was terra nullius had achieved almost gospel status, but by the late 1970s it was becoming untenable in light of the calls for Aboriginal land rights. It was not until *Mabo* case in 1992 that the High Court of Australia rejected the assumption of terra nullius – but only in regard to Indigenous rights to land.

The *Mabo* decision found that the common law of Australia depended on a discriminatory denigration of the Indigenous inhabitants, their social organisation and their customs. To continue to embrace this notion of terra nullius would perpetuate injustice, said the court. However, the recognition of native title could not overturn the doctrine of tenure of the Australian legal system in respect to land ownership. The high court also affirmed that the acquisition of sovereignty of the Australian continent was an act of state and could not be challenged in an Australian court.[2] While Australian courts are prepared to entertain Indigenous claims for land rights within the framework of the common law they will not entertain any claims that question colonial 'settlement' because to do so would upset the legal justification for the assertion of British sovereignty.

The political and policy framework
While government policy has provided opportunities for Indigenous recognition, it has largely not been able to accommodate Indigenous aspirations for self-determination. This is because parliament and government agencies are steeped in assumptions of terra nullius. Over the course of history, Australian institutions have opposed, undermined or dismissed Indigenous claims for recognition on the basis of false assumptions about Indigenous people.

In the colonial era of the 1800s, Aboriginal people were considered inferior and a doomed race who would die out or be biologically absorbed into the broader white population. British humanitarian reformers recommended a system of protection; however, this protection became an elaborate system of control and oppression. Despite the harshness of policies, Aboriginal people in Coranderrk, an Aboriginal reserve in the colonial state of Victoria, were able to assert their claim to land, highlight their grievances and challenge the policies of protection. They showed that they were equal to any person in the colony through their determination to achieve a level of self-management and self-sufficiency by farming the land. However, power rested with the Aborigines Protection Board, who considered Aboriginal people inferior and their aspirations to become self-determining a threat, and so the Board undermined the Coranderrk struggle for recognition of their rights and to retain their reserve land.

In the late 1930s in New South Wales, the Aborigines Protection Board held enormous power and control over the lives of Aboriginal people, either forcing them off reserves into towns for assimilation into white society or imprisoning them on reserves for 'civilisation' training. This also included taking children away to become indentured labour for whites. Activists such as Bill Ferguson, Jack Patten and others used the white Australian celebration of the 150th anniversary of the landing of the British First Fleet to stage a Day of Mourning conference in Sydney to highlight Aboriginal grievances against the policies of protection and to be treated equally. But newspapers dismissed their claims and the New South Wales government largely ignored their demands. While Prime Minister Joe Lyon and the Commonwealth minister for the interior met with the activists – who presented their proposed national Aboriginal policy – the prime minister was reluctant to act because the states controlled Aboriginal affairs.

By the late 1930s the policy of protection was considered to have failed and so by the 1950s a national policy of assimilation was confirmed, whereby Aboriginal people would transition into white society. The assimilation policy considered Aboriginal people inferior and did not recognise Aboriginal culture or traditional rights to land. The assumption was that Aboriginal society had nothing to offer and therefore assimilation would transition them into a 'superior civilisation'. In 1963 the Yolngu people in Arnhem Land in the Northern Territory were regarded as inferior and unintelligent but they drew on their cultural values to challenge the imposition of a bauxite mine on their traditional lands and to assert ownership of land and protection of their culture. The Yolngu challenged the assimilation policy and the decisions of the Commonwealth government by petitioning the Commonwealth parliament to assert their rights but they were not able to gain recognition of land ownership.

The Yolngu struggle resonated with a new generation of Aboriginal activists who emerged in the late 1960s and early 1970s. They staged an Aboriginal Embassy protest on the lawns of what is now Old Parliament House in Canberra, challenging the assimilation policy and focusing attention on the lack of recognition of Aboriginal rights to land and self-determination. The Commonwealth government believed that Aboriginal people would transition into white society through a focus on employment, education and enterprise development. The government also believed that Aboriginal people had no legal or moral rights to land. Establishing the Aboriginal Embassy defied parliamentary authority and embarrassed the government, who passed legislation to evict the embassy from the lawns of Parliament House.

In December 1972 the newly elected Whitlam Labor government replaced the assimilation policy with a policy of self-determination that promoted self-management, self-reliance and tackling social disadvantage. Aboriginal affairs became the responsibility of the national government and Indigenous people were provided with advisory representative capacity in policy-making at the national level. However, there was a firm belief in government that Indigenous people lacked sovereignty or any form of political authority, placing limits on Indigenous aspirations for self-determination. Issues such as national land rights and a treaty emerged on the policy agenda. But the federal government backtracked on fulfilling those promises. The failure of government would provide the impetus for a process of reconciliation in the 1990s.

When the high court handed down its *Mabo* decision in June 1992, hostile and racially charged political and public responses would dominate the public debate. Native title was considered a threat to the Australian system of land law, to economic interests, to Australian national and sovereign interests as well as a threat to the identity of Anglo-Australians. State governments and industry groups pressured for extinguishment of native title. For Indigenous leaders, however, the *Mabo* judgement laid the basis for a post-colonial settlement. But the Commonwealth government did not accept this premise, choosing to interpret native title as a land management issue for the states.

In 1993 when the Commonwealth government legislated the *Mabo* decision, it was influenced by an extinguishment approach to protect economic and private property interests by restricting native title. Indigenous leaders sought dialogue and formal negotiation with the government. While Prime Minister Paul Keating was open to dialogue and negotiation with Indigenous leaders, the outcome for Indigenous people was less than satisfactory because, while the legislation recognised native title, it was more about advancing commercial titles and providing security for existing land titles. Nevertheless, it was a turning point in Australian history because Prime Minister Keating's moral approach created the space for Indigenous representatives to be heard and respected within the law-making process. But this moment in political history has never been replicated, as the political environment in Australia changed in 1996.

A backlash followed with the election of the Howard federal Liberal–National coalition government in 1996. The Howard government promoted the false narrative that Indigenous self-determination as well as Indigenous institutions, programmes and services had failed over the previous two decades, therefore necessitating assimilationist and coercive government intervention. Among other things, Prime Minister John Howard and his government abandoned the policy of self-determination, dismantled national Indigenous representation, undertook a military intervention into Northern Territory Aboriginal communities, undermined Indigenous authority and political voices, placed tighter controls on local Indigenous organisations, eroded native title by amending the Native Title Act, derailed the formal reconciliation process and reshaped Indigenous rights towards an individual responsibility paradigm. The upheavals of Indigenous affairs during the Howard decade still reverberate today.

Beyond terra nullius thinking

History shows that terra nullius thinking has shaped an influential intellectual framework, which is reflected in various assumptions, attitudes, opinions and practices in respect to Indigenous people. This intellectual framework influences public decision-making and underlies the resistance to respecting Indigenous people and recognising their rights. Governments, politicians, public decision-makers and the influential public have had difficulties transcending their ingrained thinking about Indigenous people.

Indigenous Australians have prior and inherent cultural and political rights, which should necessitate a unique constitutional and political relationship with Australian governments. But this relationship is not recognised by governments. As a minority group, Indigenous people must rely on the goodwill of political parties, the compassion of politicians and the compassion of the Australian public for recognition and protection of their rights. While there have been instances of goodwill where Indigenous rights were recognised and promoted, progress is piecemeal and gains are easily undone, or deliberately undermined by unsympathetic governments. Indigenous people do not have equal access to or influence over government policy and decision-making and are consistently on the losing side of majority decision-making processes. There are many Australians who want a transformed relationship with Indigenous people and who support justice for Indigenous people; however, there is a lack of majority public and political support.

Edmund Rice had a special gift of power and influence that he used for the benefit and good of others in an oppressed and dominated society. He used his wealth, power and influence to benefit the poor, oppressed and dispossessed. His values of presence, compassion and liberation are integral to the work of the Edmund Rice Centre in Sydney, Australia. The Edmund Rice Centre urges solidarity with those who are disadvantaged, marginalised and excluded to build relationships of mutual respect, trust and accountability. This enables a compassionate response, which awakens us to our responsibilities and compels us to take action to address injustice because justice is the social manifestation of compassion.

These values are applicable to achieving a transformed relationship between the Australian nation and Indigenous people. It is necessary to change the cultural and political beliefs that have been inherited from the colonial past. This demands reflection and understanding based on compassion, accepting responsibility and rectifying injustices. Australians must first understand the genesis of their thinking in order to move forward in a transformed relationship with Indigenous people. This means examining and reflecting on deeply held assumptions and beliefs. The conversations will be difficult but are necessary for the betterment of the Australian nation.

Indigenous Australians have provided a way forward in the Uluru 'Statement from the Heart' from 2017.[3] Developed by Indigenous people, it is a call to the Australian population for compassion and justice. It has three key elements:

1. Enshrining a First Nations Voice in the Australian Constitution.
2. The establishment of a Makarrata Commission by legislation to supervise agreement-making between governments and First Nations.
3. The Makarrata Commission overseeing truth-telling about Australia's history and colonisation.

However, the constitutional recognition of a First Nation Voice can only be granted by a majority of Australians in a majority of states that vote in a referendum. The Australian people will decide on whether they recognise a First Nation Voice in the Constitution. In that regard it is critical for Australians to use their power, privilege and influence to stand in solidarity with Indigenous people.

Reflection
- *Reading this chapter, what did you learn about how Indigenous people are treated in Australia and how did you react?*
- *How do you think deeply ingrained assumptions and prejudices can be challenged and dislodged in a society?*
- *Are there peoples in your own country that have endured, and*

still endure, exclusion and discrimination because of their difference? How do you feel about that?

Endnotes

1. Although the preferred term to use is 'Aboriginal and Torres Strait Islander peoples', I use the terms 'Indigenous' and 'Aboriginal' interchangeably throughout this chapter.
2. *Mabo and Others v The State of Queensland* (No. 2) [1992] High Court of Australia 23; (1992) 175 Commonwealth Law Report, 1.
3. Commonwealth of Australia, 'Uluru Statement from the Heart', *Final Report of the Referendum Council*, 30 June 2017, Canberra, ACT: Department of Prime Minister and Cabinet. Available at https://www.referendumcouncil.org.au/final-report.html; accessed 25 May 2022.

REFUGEES AND RACISM: NOW IS NOT THE TIME TO BE SILENT

Phil Glendenning

When Edmund Rice opened the North Richmond Street School in Dublin, Irish independence leader Daniel O'Connell laid the foundation stone watched by some hundred thousand people. It was an amazing crowd given that Dublin's entire population in 1828 was only a few hundred thousand. Clearly, Edmund was engaged in the world. His was not a cloistered faith. He saw the unjust Penal Laws of Ireland and their impact on the poor.

Ireland of the twenty-first century is a long way from that of the Penal Laws era, yet poverty and systemic injustice remain stubborn features of life on planet Earth. The struggle for human rights continues, Indigenous rights remain to be fully achieved, climate change is an existential threat, discrimination on the grounds of race remain unresolved in many parts of the world, and the world still reels in the wake of the Covid-19 pandemic.

It would be understandable to close down, to focus inwards on protecting what is ours and those closest to us. At this point in history, Edmund Rice people cannot limit ourselves to that. Our mission takes us in another direction – outwards.

A divided, fearful and unwelcoming world

In recent times, too many nations are turning inwards. Walls are going up internationally where there should be bridges. The same isolationism seen with Brexit in the UK and the policies of Donald Trump in the US has yet to play out, as racism, anti-intellectualism, misogyny and distortions of truth are drawn upon by politicians the world over. Across Europe in recent years, a wave of hyper-nationalist politicians has weakened the rule of law by populist appeal to fear – Geert Wilders in the Netherlands, Marine Le Pen in France, Viktor Orbán in Hungary. In Brazil, we saw the Amazon-burning and pandemic-denying policies of Jair Bolsonaro, and in the Philippines we witnessed the war on truth, women and simple good taste waged by Rodrigo Duterte. The statistics are staggering. As of November 2021, the United Nations High Commissioner for Refugees (UNHCR) reported that there are 84 million forcibly displaced people in the world – people fleeing persecution, conflict, violence, or human rights violations.[1] Of these, 26.6 million are refugees living in foreign lands and 48 million are internally displaced peoples. These figures do not account for the ongoing refugee crisis stemming from the Russian invasion of Ukraine, which has seen a further 5.6 million refugees displaced to foreign countries and more than 7 million displaced within Ukraine.[2] On average, thirty-seven thousand new people are forced to flee their homes *every day*. Tragically, almost half the refugees in the world are children under eighteen years of age. Most of these refugees are not taken in by the rich industrialised nations of Europe, North America and Australia. Eighty-five per cent of refugees are taken in by developing countries. The UNHCR is inadequately funded to support the people who need protection and too often the people the UNHCR is mandated to protect are rejected by other countries.

Participation or silence?

The vision of Edmund Rice calls us to something different – to walk together in companionship with people who seek protection and to afford critical attention to the larger movements in society and the world, over which refugees have no control but which nevertheless shape their lives. The lives of refugees depend on what Australian Jesuit Andrew Hamilton calls:

> the resolution of that larger choice between dystopia and hospitality. ... They call for the small kindnesses of support and advocacy, along with visits and consultations for the legal and other agencies that have stuck by them and given them hope. They also call for critical attention to the world which we by participation or by silence will shape.[3]

So Edmund Rice people have a choice to make – to participate or be silent. Pope Francis has denounced this 'globalization of indifference' and said 'a painful truth' is that 'our world is daily more and more elitist, more cruel towards the excluded'. He reminded people of goodwill worldwide that 'as Christians, we cannot be indifferent to the tragedy of old and new forms of poverty, to the bleak isolation, contempt and discrimination experienced by those who do not belong to "our" group,' and added, 'we cannot remain insensitive, our hearts deadened, before the misery of so many innocent people. We must not fail to weep. We must not fail to respond.'[4] Pope Francis makes it clear that what refugees are looking for is, put simply, peace. They seek a peace that is free of racism, discrimination, dispossession, incarceration and fear. In my country of Australia, it is the same aspiration Aboriginal and Torres Strait Islander peoples seek, to find an

105

end to the injustices of colonialism and find a place of peace in their own land.

First Nations peoples and the aspiration for peace
The aspiration from Australia's First Nations peoples, for peace in their homeland and for an end to all forms of injustice, racism and discrimination, was beautifully presented to the nation at Uluru in May 2017, in the 'Statement from the Heart'.[5] It was a cry for peace. It was an echo of the cries for freedom from refugees incarcerated for nearly seven years in detention centres in Manus, Nauru and Port Moresby. It can be heard in refugee camps in northern Kenya, in Jordan, Syria, Turkey and in the forty-two displaced peoples' camps that ring Kabul in Afghanistan. It is the same heart-rending cry – human beings pleading for peace, for themselves, their families, and their country. Australian Aboriginal people have been involved in an ongoing fight for freedom and peace since the first boatload of unauthorised arrivals landed in Sydney in 1788. Australian Aboriginal Senator Patrick Dodson said:

> I was born before the 1967 referendum, when we as Aboriginal people were not even counted in the census of this country, when this government did not have any power to make laws for Aboriginal people because it was excluded by the crafters of our Constitution in 1901. The whole battle for recognition – for freedom to enjoy the basics of being a citizen – in this nation had to be fought for.[6]

The 'basics of being a citizen' remain under threat. If you listen closely to the language common to public debate in many countries, you could be forgiven for thinking that we all live together in an *economy* rather than a *society*. This is important because members of a society are *citizens*, and they have *rights* and they have *responsibilities*. However, members of an economy are *customers* or *consumers*, with *choices* – dependent on how much wealth they have access to. Money comes before people.

The legacy of Reaganomics and Thatcherism
This paradigm shift from a society to an economy – begun in Thatcher's Britain and Reagan's USA in the 1980's – has been accompanied by shifts in language. For example, travellers on planes are increasingly not referred to as *passengers*; they are referred to as *customers*. Banks no longer provide *services*; they sell *products*. And those who reside in the care of psychiatric institutions are no longer *patients* or *residents*; everyone is a *client* (what are they purchasing?). Moreover, those who live in a *society* are valued inherently for *who they are*, as human beings with inalienable rights; in an economy we value people for *what they can do*, for their utility or production value. And once we base our relationships and interactions on economics primarily rather than on humanity, it becomes easier to treat people in inhuman ways. It becomes easier to turn away from the refugee, to blame those who have been made poor for their poverty and to deny climate change. The paradigm needs to shift back.

Essential to that shift, therefore, is a need to reclaim the language and fundamentally put humanity and the planet back in the picture. The language we use matters, because when we strip back the language we reveal the *assumptions* underpinning decisions, and when we strip back the assumptions underpinning decisions we reveal the *values* decisions are based on. The values broadly at work are not the values Pope Francis calls for in *Laudato Si'*, and they are not the values of Edmund Rice. If we are not attentive to the words we use and the assumptions and values they represent, as Senator Dodson has said in the Australian Parliament, this enables and emboldens 'an ideological creep back to bigotry and to racism'.[7] And, as we have learned from the twentieth century, racism was too often the pre-cursor to conflict, to war, and even to genocide.

The long shadow of racism
In 2020 across the world people took to the streets to defend the sanctity of human life and to reject racism. Racism is based in a fundamental inability to see the world from the perspective of 'the other'. Sometimes this racism does not need to be aggressive, abusive or angry. It can be quietly, complacently apathetic or just indifferent. Racism is not natural to human beings, but rather is something that is created, nurtured, taught and encouraged. As Northern Ireland politician David Ervine put it at an Australian Treaty Conference: 'I can smell racism. It doesn't grow wild in a field. It is tended in a window box'.[8]

The point here is simple: in a world where peace remains elusive, where so many people are displaced, where racism is real, the words we use count. Language matters. And our actions must follow suit. As Patrick Dodson said: 'If [we] cannot stand up for the weakest, the poorest and those who are most vulnerable because of their race, their ethnicity or their beliefs, then we have become a very sad replication of what democracy is about'.[9] Similarly, we will have failed to live up to the outward-looking vision and mission of Edmund Rice.

In the eighteenth century, the German philosopher Immanuel Kant proposed that human beings are never a means to an end; they are an end in themselves.[10] His words loudly and boldly echo down the centuries in stark contrast to

Australia's treatment of asylum seekers and refugees on Nauru and Manus Island – detention centres that have imprisoned refugees for up to eight years for seeking Australia's protection. The human cost of this policy and practice has been simply shocking. At the Edmund Rice Centre in Sydney we know a young man who read one morning that the government was preparing to ban all boat arrivals from ever entering Australia under any circumstances. An asylum seeker who had come to Australia by boat, he went straight to his bathroom and swallowed a bottle of sleeping pills. He survived, but the hope that sustained him for so long during his escape from the Taliban to the dangerous journey to Australia has been extinguished. He is one of the thirty thousand asylum seekers in the community without rights or resolution to his case. The devastating impact of these policies of incarceration and punishment on innocent people simply has to stop.

Inhuman treatment
Simply put, today we treat asylum seekers and refugees who have arrived by boat as if we were at war with them. Amnesty International reports that Australia's system discriminates against, punishes and in some cases 'tortures' people who come seeking safety and protection, and who instead can remain in detention for up to eight years.[11] This was certainly the case for Mahomood (name changed), and her eleven-year-old daughter (who has now spent more than half her life on Nauru). Although recognised as a refugee, Mahomood lives on a recurrent three-year visa – a Nauruan passport lists her identity as 'refugee'. Mahomood and her daughter lived in a remote camp. She was too scared to go out for food following an attack by two men on motorbikes as she walked to town to collect groceries. Her life in recent years has been spent in a two-by-four-metre, plywood-walled, tin-roofed shack.

She says she has spent years crying, because all her hope is gone. The tragic irony of this is that Mahomood came on the same boat as her brother. Today he lives in Sydney's south, married to an Australian woman and they are expecting their first baby.

The current policy of punishment and deterrence has moved Australia further away from engaging in the real global challenge of assisting the almost 100 million people who are displaced. Last year there were 26.6 million people recognised as refugees among displaced people internationally. Less than one per cent of those found to be refugees were re-settled. A fixation with securing borders results in an inability to engage meaningfully in working with the international community to tackle the root causes of displacement and to ensure the people that do flee their country can live with dignity in the places they flee to. It is vital that parents can work legally, that children can access schools and that healthcare is freely available. Also, all research indicates that when refugees receive permanent protection they make a sustained positive contribution to the life of their new nation. These 26 million refugees – the population of Australia – are not just numbers. They are human beings. They are brothers, fathers, sisters, mothers and friends. More than half are children. They include Mahomood and her daughter.

This is not the time for silence
The starting point for putting all of this to rights is in listening to the voices that for too long have been suppressed or hidden. To this end, I recently came across a poem penned anonymously by a young Iranian asylum seeker who spent a number of years in mandatory detention after arriving in Australia by boat:

I do not know
what will happen after I die.
I do not want to know.
But I would like the Potter to make a whistle
from the clay of my throat.
May this whistle fall into the hands
of a cheeky and naughty child
and the child to blow hard on the whistle continuously
with all the suppressed and silent air of his lungs
and disrupt the sleep
of those who seem dead
to my cries.[12]

We, as Edmund Rice people, must proclaim to that asylum seeker, and all others who seek protection only to be met by cruelty, that we are not dead to their cries. Our commitment as Edmund Rice people to presence and compassion means that we must listen to those with lived experience as a first and fundamental step towards their liberation. We must get to know them and assist them to find their voice. This will go a long way towards the liberation of all of us from the bonds of systemic discrimination and institutional racism. In doing this, we must be careful not to repeat the sins of colonialism and allow our good intentions to get in the way of justice and solidarity. In the words of a wise Aboriginal woman from northern Australia, Lila Watson, on encountering a group of mission workers, 'if you have come to help me, you are wasting your time. But if you have come because your liberation is bound up with mine, then let us walk together'.[13]

Now is not the time to be silent. Martin Luther King Jr once famously said that silence is betrayal.[14] Today the marginalised and displaced peoples of the world, and the very planet we share, must not have their cries met with the deadening silence of indifference. The sleep of those who are dead to these cries needs to be disturbed on a nightly basis. The words of British journalist Laurie Penny, writing for the *New Statesman* about Europe, seem ever more apt today, and not just for the European continent:

> Migration does change society, although far less so than, for example, technology, economic austerity, escalating inequality, globalisation or climate change. But the greatest threat to our 'way of life', if there has ever been such a thing on this vast and varied continent, is not that someday you or I might be sitting on a bus and hear someone speaking Pashto or Tigrinya [or Dari or Arabic]. The threat is that we will swallow the public narrative that immigrants, people from non-European countries are less human than the rest of us, that they think and feel less, that they matter less. Many people in western countries are quite capable of sitting calmly in the bubbling water of cultural bigotry until it boils away every shred of compassion we have left. That's the real threat to our 'way of life'.[15]

The gift we have received from Edmund Rice is a counter-cultural belief that compassion for others is not a form of weakness. In fact, compassion is our greatest civilising strength. The time has come for us to play to that strength, to demonstrate it, and to mobilise it. This is essential if the example of Edmund Rice is to remain relevant and lived out in our times.

The good news is that history tells us that these changes we seek are not simply idealistically naïve. No one would have believed it in the nineteenth century if told that one day women would get the vote. No one would have believed at times in the twentieth century if told that the Soviet Union would end peacefully, that the Berlin Wall would come down, that apartheid in South Africa would end, and that Nelson Mandela would be freed from jail and become president of the country. No one would have believed if told that a black man would one day be president in the White House or that many governments around the world would establish departments of the environment. Positive change is real when people get organised into movements, into peoples' movements – like the environment movement, the anti-apartheid movement, the women's rights movement, the anti-nuclear movement and the peace movement. And in recent times we have seen the climate change movement across the world led by a sixteen-year-old schoolgirl. All of these movements are characterised by people gathering together in loose and shifting coalitions to take collective action around shared values. Now is the time for the Edmund Rice movement. The time is now and we are here. As Martin Luther King Jr said, 'the arc of the moral universe is long but it bends towards justice'.[16] What he didn't say, however, was that the arc needs people to do the bending. That is our task, and it is our challenge. It was put best by Robert F. Kennedy in an address at the University of Cape Town, South Africa:

> Only earthbound man still clings to the dark and poisoning superstition that his world is bounded by the nearest hill, his universe ends at the river's shore, his common humanity is enclosed in the tight circle of those who share his town or his views and the colour of his skin.[17]

Surely today it is the task of the Edmund Rice movement across the world to, as Br Philip Pinto once put it, 'work together to strip the last remnants of that cruel and ancient belief from the fabric of humankind'. So we seek a world where the needs of the poor take priority over the wants of the rich; where the freedom of the weak takes priority over the liberty of the powerful; and where the access of the excluded in society takes priority over the preservation of an order that does not include them. When we act on these preferential options, we will attract criticism – at times, persecution and calumny. It happened to Edmund and if we are to engage effectively with the world at this time of history, it will happen to us. Good. Because when you are over the target, you have to expect flak. It's part of the deal. So let's reclaim the language, spread the truth around, bend the arc of history in favour of justice – and blow loudly on those clay whistles.

Reflection

- *Half the refugees in the world are under eighteen years of age and 84 per cent of refugees are taken in by developing countries. How do you react to statistics like this?*
- *In your own country, which comes first, the people or the economy? What did the pandemic reveal? What does the language used by politicians and the media reveal? Of the 26 million people recognised in one year as refugees, 1% were resettled. What does this reveal?*
- *Do you think that British journalist Laurie Penny is in any way overstating it when she says that the biggest threat to our 'way of life' is the narrative that immigrants are less human and think, feel and matter less than the rest of us?*

Endnotes

1. See the UNHCR's Refugee Population Statistics Database, 10 November 2021. Available at https://www.unhcr.org/refugee-statistics/; accessed 25 May 2022.
2. See UNHCR, 'Ukraine Emergency', updated 5 July 2022. Available at https://www.unhcr.org/en-ie/ukraine-emergency.html; accessed 9 July 2022.
3. Andrew Hamilton, 'Reflecting on this Refugee Week', *Eureka Street*, 11 June 2020. Available at https://www.eurekastreet.com.au/article/reflecting-on-this-refugee-week; accessed 25 May 2022.
4. Pope Francis, Homily at Holy Mass on the Occasion of the World Day of Migrants and Refugees, 29 September 2019. Available at https://www.vatican.va/content/francesco/en/homilies/2019/documents/papa-francesco_20190929_omelia-migranti.html; accessed 25 May 2022.
5. Commonwealth of Australia, 'Uluru Statement from the Heart', *Final Report of the Referendum Council*, 30 June 2017, Canberra, ACT: Department of Prime Minister and Cabinet. Available at https://www.referendumcouncil.org.au/final-report.html; accessed 25 May 2022.
6. Patrick Dodson, quoted in Katharine Murphy, 'Racial Discrimination Act debate a "creep back to bigotry", says Pat Dodson', *The Guardian*, 24 November 2016. Available at https://www.theguardian.com/australia-news/2016/nov/24/racial-discrimination-act-debate-a-creep-back-to-bigotry-says-pat-dodson; accessed 25 May 2022.
7. Ibid.
8. David Ervine, Address at the National Treaty Conference, Canberra, 27–9 August 2002, organised by Australians for Native Title and Reconciliation (ANTaR).
9. Patrick Dodson, op. cit.
10. Cf. Immanuel Kant, *Grounding of the Metaphysics of Morals*, trans. J.W. Ellington, Indianapolis/Cambridge: Hackett, p. 36, n. 429.
11. Amnesty International, 'Australia: Appalling abuse, neglect of refugees on Nauru', press release, 2 August 2016. Available at https://www.amnesty.org/en/latest/news/2016/08/australia-abuse-neglect-of-refugees-on-nauru/; accessed 25 May 2022.
12. Anonymous, 'Make a whistle from my throat', as quoted in Emma Cox 'The Citation of Injury: Regarding the Exceptional Body', *Journal of Australian Studies*, Vol. 33, No. 4, December 2009, pp. 459–72.

13 Quoted in Karen House, *Reflections for Spring Break Mission Trips*, Karenhousecw.org, spring 2001. Available at www.karenhousecw.org/documents/ReflectionManual.pdf; accessed 30 May 2022.

14 Martin Luther King Jr, 'Beyond Vietnam: A Time to Break Silence', speech delivered 4 April 1967, quoted in 'When Silence is Betrayal', RethinkingSchools.org. Available at www.rethinkingschools.org/special-collections/when-silence-is-betrayal; accessed 30 May 2022.

15 Laurie Penny, 'Europe shouldn't worry about migrants. It should worry about creeping fascism', *New Statesman*, 14 August 2015. Available at www.newstatesman.com/politics/2015/08/europe-shouldn-t-worry-about-migrants-it-should-worry-about-creeping-fascism; accessed 30 May 2022.

16 Martin Luther King Jr, 'Remaining Awake Through a Great Revolution', speech given at the National Cathedral, 31 March 1968.

17 Robert F. Kennedy, 'Day of Affirmation' address, University of Cape Town, Cape Town, South Africa, 6 June 1996. Available at https://www.jfklibrary.org/learn/about-jfk/the-kennedy-family/robert-f-kennedy/robert-f-kennedy-speeches/day-of-affirmation-address-university-of-capetown-capetown-south-africa-june-6-1966; accessed 30 May 2022.

EDUCATION, EXCLUSION AND HOPE

Don O'Leary

> The time is now! The place is here! You are the people! ... Dare to enter my Mystery and become hope for the world. Risk being different! Risk leaping and falling! Remember, falling is the privilege of the living and even as you encounter loss, fear, despair, and death know I have been there before you and will be with you always. Trust me.[1]

The above quote, from the day I first read it, has always struck a deep chord with me. The Christian Brothers' Congregation Chapter in Munnar, India, in 2008 happened two years after I became director of the Cork Life Centre and it has real meaning for the work we do both with children and families. In writing this piece I have reflected on this message and how applicable it is to the stories that unfold in our every day in Cork behind the red door. We are hugely privileged to work with amazing young people and families who through different circumstances find themselves on the margins of Irish society. These circumstances can involve deprivation and prejudice, and can range from incarceration to mental illness, addiction, economic disadvantage including homelessness, direct provision and, indeed, every type of trauma and loss that the human spirit can encounter.

People often characterise what I have described above as a burden or a depressing space in which to work, however volunteers, staff and students of the Cork Life Centre have risked taking the leap and in doing so have developed a community of learning and care. All of the above problems are man-made, and we have somehow built a society that perpetuates them. Given this, we can also focus on a more hopeful message that we can tear them down and build our society and communities anew. This is what we have tried to do in our small way in Sunday's Well in Cork – to build a community where all are welcome, cherished, celebrated and no one is labelled, excluded or shamed for their journey to our doors.

Looking out the window of the Cork Life Centre
Over two hundred years ago Edmund Rice looked out his window, saw a world that didn't sit right with him and took a leap of faith. But for that leap of faith I might not be sitting looking out the window of the Cork Life Centre writing these words. I want to take that window as the vantage point from which I tell stories of exclusion, education and hope but ultimately of exceptional young people that have inspired and continue to inspire me.

A tall, seemingly cocky and self-assured young man makes his way up the drive to meet me. He's well dressed and has a certain swagger – he presents himself in a way that would land him with the stereotypical label of an 'early school-leaver'. What I am really looking at, of course, is a very frightened and vulnerable child who has found all kinds of creative and resilient ways of masking pain, loss, fear and exclusion. But I would learn all this little by little, time being so important for a young person who has been given no reason to trust people in a world that has shown little kindness. In his life, the two people you are supposed to rely on most (your parents) had been lost to him at a young age – one through death and the other through incarceration. Then the ensuing pain and terror of being placed in care and uprooted from what was left of his family, his friends and school, his remaining safe space. In time we would hear more of his journey, his rebellion against the injustice of his life and what it had become, his confusion about what was right or wrong in a world where he felt like he was always punished.

I'm looking out my car window as I approach the gates of a juvenile detention facility. I am happy to be able to visit but I still wish I didn't have to. In the short time I have known him, things have really spiralled. This can happen fast when you live in a care setting where the police are called when you abscond because you don't want to be there, when you 'act out' and cause damage because you cannot possibly manage your thoughts and feelings, when you take drugs and drink alcohol to block out all the things that have happened and are happening that you just can't cope with.

I'm sitting by the window of the visitor's room at a residential drug treatment centre. He is out now and working hard on making positive changes – accessing drug and mental health services, trying to keep safe while he works through a world of trauma. I feel privileged to be here but I'm angry because it hasn't taken very much for our team and others who have worked with this young person to see the real him – the person that could flourish if there weren't so many odds stacked against them and a system that often exacerbates these.

Seeing what success really looks like
Even on that first day before he had dropped any of the swagger, I met a child who wanted a chance and an education. I

witnessed and acknowledged countless moments of kindness, support and understanding provided to peers. I saw him take the leap on so many occasions – things that might seem small but are huge when you've never been taught or shown how to open up, trust people, be trusted and have real, authentic relationships. In truth, these are unimaginable feats made possible by having the right place and pace to do so.

I'm sitting now in a public gallery with tears in my eyes. They are not my first tears though. There have been others born of fear, frustration, even despair, but today it is overwhelming pride. I watch a young adult stand and tell his story from start to finish – of an almost impossible journey from a seemingly inescapable place to the success he has achieved (and is achieving) today. In the room, there are people with influence who need to hear it. He has put his words together with some support from our team – it is the first time he has been able or dared to do so. The silence is palpable. Everyone listening is affected. They are getting to see what we have always seen: a child (now a young man) and a person who is not a label, a statistic or a social problem to be solved. When he finishes his speech, everyone wants to speak to him. They want to congratulate him for his resilience, his commitment, his determination and his courage. They want to validate his journey. And this is the most powerful moment I have experienced with this young man so far, in what has been and continues to be a challenging journey. More powerful than that will be when he passes his leaving certificate exams and completes his secondary education. I am prouder in this moment than I have ever been because I know his motivation in making this difficult speech. It is to speak for system change and to speak for the young people who have not survived the many traumas he has.

So, what has he taught us about education? Surely that, like many, he has learned more outside the classroom than within – learning through his relationships and experiences what kind of place the world was. Much of this we wish he hadn't learned, known or seen, but for the time in which he knew us, even when he was absent from the classroom or the community, he also learned that some people stay, that they can sit with you through the pain and the worst times and not turn away, and that they can hold you in their hearts even when you are not physically there. They can also hold hope for you when you have none left. A leaving cert is a piece of paper that will hopefully open doors that were once shut firmly, but surely the experience and proof that there are people in the world who will care about you unconditionally might sow the seeds of a flickering but powerful hope – because if we can learn to hope, and maybe from there to dream, then nothing is outside our reach.

An apparent 'failure' who becomes the teacher she always was

I'm looking out the window again. It's early, before 8 a.m., and I can see a young woman making her way to our red door. Her movements are laboured and deliberate, she is hunched over as if winded or trying to make herself invisible. It's ninety minutes before classes commence, but this has become her pattern. She makes her way to a classroom and sits on the floor out of sight with her back to the wall. She's sweating, she's pale and she's desperately hoping no one will engage with her as she works to regulate her anxiety ahead of the start of the day. If someone should enter the room unannounced she will jump in fright and she will always apologise – she is always sorry and always terrified of not doing the 'right' thing. Much later – indeed years later – when we can finally talk, she is urged to stop apologising for existing, to take up her space in the world, to look for the support she deserves.

Academically she is a high achiever and a perfectionist, however the thought of sitting for an exam reduces her to a panic attack. She is not your stereotypical 'early school-leaver'. In a lot of ways she was the perfect student, internalising all the messages of the education system that bring Patrick Pearse's essay 'The Murder Machine' to mind. In this quite remarkable work, written in 1912, the great Irish patriot, poet and teacher outlined his radical pedagogical vision and attacked the then current 'filthy' utilitarian education as a 'lifeless thing without a soul' that turns people into 'mere things' for sale.[2] For her, the mainstream was just that, something that had been breaking her down until her family said 'no more'.

I'm looking through the window of the classroom door again, checking if she is OK. It has become an art and a dance demonstrating care without crowding. She is seated this time in a crowd; she looks terrified, but she is there. She's at a launch for a book she has written about her journey so far. Writing has proved a vehicle to communicate with us and with others – to start talking and healing. Little notes conveying distress were the kindling that fanned slow and steady flames that burned into real conversations about early loss and bereavement, about the unrelenting worry for family, about self-hatred and not feeling comfortable in one's skin, about communicating pain through self-harm, about thoughts of suicide.

I'm at the kitchen window now, a number of years have passed but we've always kept in touch. They are on their way, early as always, still a little nervous but with a quiet and building confidence. They are a teacher now, not a student, degrees achieved with plans for further study. And I am full of pride and wonder at all they will bring to their new role on the other side of the desk. The 'experts' think they know who 'early school-leavers' are, what they need, what they can and can't achieve. A focus on practical and vocational subjects is a part of this, a rhythm and routine to keep young people off the street is another. Here was a young person at no risk of getting into 'trouble' or offending, overly compliant, academically capable with a pursuit of perfection. None of the above was needed but rather patience, persistence, love and a refusal to accept that being 'fine' is good enough. A journey to self-discovery and acceptance was started with the leap of writing that first note, with taking the risk to start a conversation. Education policies don't often tell us how important time and trust and conversations are. Perhaps these things are too vague and immeasurable, or perhaps too human?

Removing the dark mask and revealing the beauty
I'm at the window again; winter is whipping around us and the young person I see fits the climate. She looks sullen, moody and dark – dark clothes, dark make-up and generally disinterested. Her body language as she gets out of her mother's car tells me she doesn't seem to want to be here, but nevertheless we meet and agree to work together. Over the next few months I saw her less from the window than I would have liked – her attendance was patchy at best, and even when she was present it was in body only, not really engaging. Perhaps she really didn't want to be here; this was her right and would be respected but there's usually more to it than that. Often young people can't rather than won't show up and you have to keep the door open when people's experience is to have had them closed. The dark persona continued to pervade and could be interpreted as uncooperative, but we persisted demonstrating that we noticed and cared when she didn't show up. Slowly but surely conversations started to happen and she started to show up more often but remained committed to showing

that her education was not that important to her and to not allowing anybody to get too close. Underneath the dark mask lay someone who felt quite lost and had very low self-esteem who had started to mix with a dangerous group of peers and engage in drug-taking. Anyone can seem like a friend when you are lonely and looking for a place to belong and youth can be a very lonely time for some.

Without making too much progress on what was really going on for this young person, she made the decision to repeat fifth year – her own decision and one that would pay dividends. A few months later and she is the one sitting at the window – a place where she's found more often now and rather than being late can be the morning's first arrival. She has become more quiet and withdrawn in class but in the morning at our kitchen table she writes prolifically. Later she discloses that she has been sexually assaulted. This is what she is trying to come to terms with as she sits and writes, filling notebooks and filling time. We support her to report the crime and to access the therapeutic support she needs. With what must have felt like a terrible secret out in the open, her relationship to the staff and centre flourishes. I begin to see her less often sitting alone by the window; a little group of peers is gathering around her – people who enjoy her quiet company and are happy to leave her to write and chat only occasionally. Writing becomes a huge source of strength and solace. Finding her footing, she develops a love rather than a tolerance for learning. She becomes thirsty to learn about herself and the world and takes every opportunity we offer her with both hands – even those that scare her. She completes her leaving cert and sets about finding what she is passionate about learning next. She also steadily finds her voice, becoming interested in being an advocate for young people in general and young women in particular.

Now when I look out the window she is a regular visitor. She is bright in spirit, in clothing, in energy. She is pursuing her dreams. She is still a writer, but also a dreamer full of the youthful exuberance that was hidden when we first met. And again we have been lucky to learn that even through the worst of adversity and the darkest of seasons, with support, opportunities and the right balance of challenge and comfort, hope springs and the seed will grow.

Above are just three snippets of intensely complex and individual journeys that young people took through life and education that brought them to our red doors. I can only hope that they do some justice to the young people that have inspired them – to their energy and perseverance and to their commitment to challenging themselves and taking monumental leaps of faith to engage with their education in the truest sense of the word.

Education is not simply about schooling but something completely different

Education, of course, continues to be confused with schooling. We would posit that a school is just a building; what we aspire to create instead is a community of learning. Here is the definition of education that we can live and work by:

> Education is the wise, hopeful and respectful cultivation of learning undertaken in the belief that all should have the chance to share in life. It is a process of inviting truth and possibility.

Therefore, education cannot happen unless it welcomes and embraces all. And doing so, it must involve engaging with all parts of the person and their story. By being open to that possibility, we have for twenty years forged our own

extraordinary journey and we are richer and wiser for it. But we are always learning. And here are some vital lessons:
- The world is too complex and at times too cruel for things to be black, white or indeed all in colour.
- You cannot categorise people into good and bad. We have known heroes and warriors that others might miss or classify as villains or victims.
- There are no tidy interventions with reassuring and happy endings. Things are always to be continued and often there are more forks ahead in the road.
- With support, understanding and encouragement there is always resilience and perseverance which can lead to growth, light and hope for those brave enough to take that first leap.

I want to thank those who have informed my life and work so greatly by being brave enough to take the leap with us: first and foremost our many students (present and past), but also their parents, families and of course the staff of the Cork Life Centre, mainly composed of volunteers who support and journey with our young people.

On a personal note: it is imperative that I thank our trustees, the European Province of Christian Brothers – our journey would not have been possible without them. In particular, my work has been inspired and sustained by people like Brs Paul Hendrick, Gary O'Shea and Ned Hayden, Sr Mary Flood, Cormac McArt, Rachel Lucey and Thomas Mulcahy – all who walk in the footsteps of Edmund Rice today.

In the times we live in, through the wake of Covid-19, we hear often the message that there is no movement without risk. Yet this has always applied to all who are lost, lonely, marginalised, hurt, mistreated or ignored in our society. We have always expected them to move and change and grow in ways that we fail to recognise as terrifying and impossible unless we leap more than half the way to meet them where they are, where society has placed them. We keep the faith for a world and an education system that fully recognises this idea. Until then we look out our own window and work from there.

Reflection
- *For many, education is seen simply as a means of social advancement, of 'climbing up the ladder', 'getting on in life'. Yet this notion of 'getting/moving on' leaves others behind, especially those who are disadvantaged in any way by many factors such as where they are born, what family/social upbringing they may have, talents or other advantages they may have or simply by luck itself. Life and life chances are indeed a lottery. Yet Edmund Rice saw education differently. It was not just a means of social advancement and escaping poverty. For Edmund education was about liberation and being fully human. It was about discovering self, others and God. When Don looks out the window he sees something – someone – much more important than exam grades and academic and social 'success'. Don encounters young people who are lost – even to themselves – and restores them to themselves, their families and society.*
- *Do we see education purely in terms of academic 'success' or 'failure'?*
- *Do we see the young person who is struggling as someone who should be left behind and abandoned? Or do we see them as a lost child who can – through support, compassion and love – be brought back to life?*

Endnotes

1 Christian Brothers Chapter 2008, Munnar, India, *The Spirit Moving in our Midst: Be My Disciple*, 2008. Available at http://edmundrice.net/images/Chapter/2008_The_Spirit_in_our_Midst.pdf; accessed 22 July 2022.

2 Pádraic H. Pearse, 'The Murder Machine', in *Political Writings and Speeches*, Dublin: Phoenix Publishing, 1924, pp. 5–50. Available at https://celt.ucc.ie/published/E900007-001/index.html; accessed 30 May 2022.

FOR I WAS HUNGRY AND YOU GAVE ME FOOD: FOOD BEFORE EMPOWERMENT

John McCourt

We live in an unfair world. A majority of people in some countries enjoy many of the benefits of a highly advanced technological society. A majority of people in other countries can only dream of having such benefits. A survey by Oxfam in 2019 revealed that a mere twenty-six billionaires own as much of the world's wealth as 3.8 billion of the world's poorest people.[1] Such inequality is gross injustice, pure and simple, and flies in the face of the gospel. The Lord said that the poor will be always with us and this is only too true where African countries are concerned. Many of the people in these countries lack access to education, proper sanitation, clean water, healthcare and employment opportunities. These problems are exacerbated by the challenges presented by early marriages, teenage pregnancies and diseases such as malaria and HIV/AIDS. Add to this human trafficking and corruption as well as climate change, which poses a massive threat to people's lives and livelihoods. Now, although some people would tend to criticise the idea of providing handouts and even food for poor people, asserting that such handouts only keep people in the state of dependency, it is very difficult to stand idly by and watch people starve on one's very doorstep. Edmund Rice did not do so, Pope Francis routinely urges us not to do so and Jesus, in the gospel, leaves us to ponder such parables as that of the rich man and Lazarus (cf. Lk 16:19-31).

A province forgotten and neglected

Mongu is the capital of Western Province in the Republic of Zambia, one of ten provinces in the country. Western Province, formerly known as Barotseland, is one of the poorest regions in Zambia. It is home to the Lozi people, a proud tribe with strong traditions dating back many, many years. They have a paramount chief or king, known as the Litunga, who is greatly revered and respected by the Lozi people. Some people would say that his voice is stronger than that of the national government and holds more sway among the Lozi people, who worship the Litunga in many ways. At the time of Zambia's independence from Britain in 1964, the rulers of Barotseland, known as the Barotse Royal Establishment, were keen to remain as a protectorate of Britain rather than become part of the newly independent Zambia. However, a last-minute deal was struck and the famous Barotseland Agreement was signed, which enabled Barotseland to become part of the new Zambia, with promises of substantial financial aid among other things. Barotseland was henceforth then known as Western Province. This did not find universal favour among all the Lozi people and from time to time, even to this day, there are occasional civil disturbances orchestrated by Barotse activists looking for the old Barotseland protectorate to be restored, with the intention of breaking away from Zambia.

Western Province lies on the very outer limits of the Kalahari Desert and signs of desertification are all around to be seen. The sandy soil can be very unforgiving and makes life extremely difficult for small scale farmers. The most redeeming natural feature of Western Province is the Zambezi Floodplain which enables people to grow rice during the rainy season, if and when, the water levels are favourable. Mongu rice is always in great demand in many parts of the country. However, poor rainfall in recent successive years has made traditional subsistence farming ever more difficult. The vast majority of the people here have no access to electricity and depend on charcoal and firewood for cooking purposes. Even in some of the towns in Western Province many people can ill-afford to pay for electricity in their homes. Chopping down trees to make charcoal is very common and for some people it is their only source of income. Deforestation is playing havoc with the countryside and is impacting negatively on people's lives as climate change becomes a more visible reality in Western Province.

Lack of substantial government investment in Western Province over the years has had a serious and detrimental effect on the people of Western Province. The government is by far the largest employer in the area, employing civil servants, doctors, nurses, teachers, etc. However, unemployment levels are extremely high. Private investment is at a premium. Many bright young people follow the trend of migrating to larger urban areas in Zambia like Lusaka in Central Province or Ndola in the Copperbelt Province and thus their skills are lost to Western Province. The local government finds it quite challenging to recruit employees for public jobs as many from outside of Western Province do not relish the prospect of living in such an undeveloped and remote part of the country. Unlike other parts of Zambia, Western Province does not possess any mineral wealth and so does not attract too many outside investors. The road infrastructure throughout the province leaves much to be desired. The restrictions placed on outside investors by the interference of local chiefs and traditional headmen has deterred many would-be foreign investors over the years.

As with most Zambians, maize, and to a lesser extent cassava, makes up the staple diet of the people in Western Province. Growing maize is very difficult due to the poor quality of the soil and the ever-changing weather patterns. No longer can subsistence farmers depend on reliable annual rainfalls and so when to start planting maize has become very problematic and indeed can be something of a lottery. All of these combined factors have seen people living in rural areas struggling to survive from day to day. Food security into the future has become a real worrying issue that requires urgent government attention. Poverty levels in these areas are extremely high and drive many young people into prostitution or other forms of crime-related activity. To compound the situation there is still a high instance of HIV/AIDS infection among the younger generation. Mongu has in recent times gained the unwelcome statistic of having one of the highest HIV/AIDS infection rates in the country, this despite many NGO education programmes aimed at raising HIV/AIDS awareness. Child-headed households are not uncommon. Grandparents often take on the role of provider for their grandchildren in the absence of the parents and this proves to be a very heavy burden for so many elderly people. Alcohol abuse is very prevalent in rural areas. The alcohol consumed is very often of the illegal, homemade variety, made in very unhygienic conditions with no care given to basic sanitary standards in the brewing process.

Education and economic collapse
The Christian Brothers first came from Ireland to Mongu in 1967. They began teaching in, and administering, St John's Secondary School in Mongu, a boarding school for boys that

was founded by the Irish Capuchin Franciscans in the late 1950s. Like many other Catholic mission schools in Zambia, St John's soon gained a reputation for good discipline, hard work and academic excellence, which made the school the envy of many others in the country. The school has maintained high academic standards up to the present day, though the Christian Brothers are no longer directly involved. The school is now under the auspices of the Catholic diocese of Mongu, with dedicated lay teachers serving in key administrative roles, quite a number of whom are in fact former pupils of St John's. This ensures that the good traditions and values handed down from the foundation of the school continue to the present day. From its earliest days, many past pupils of the school have gone on to enjoy very distinguished careers in a variety of fields, including industry, education and politics, both in Zambia and overseas.

In the early 1980s, following a serious economic collapse in Zambia, which was due in the main to unwise economic and political decisions, life for a large majority of Zambians became a real struggle. Much needed government funds at that time were directed towards supporting the liberation struggles in neighbouring countries such as South Africa, Zimbabwe (formerly Rhodesia) and Namibia (formerly South-West Africa). The rising cost of living, coupled with shortages of some essential commodities, made life really challenging for many families. Schooling, for example, had become expensive and indeed unaffordable for many families. The Christian Brothers took a bold decision to phase out boarding in their schools. The majority of students in boarding schools like St John's were from relatively well-off families who lived outside of Mongu. The intention of phasing out boarding at St John's was to enable the school to cater for Mongu boys and, when the school became co-educational, girls.

The sick, the bedridden and the disabled

Evidence of the challenges faced by poorer families could be seen in the ever-growing number of callers at the Christian Brothers' house desperately seeking food or money. It was difficult for the brothers to discern who were the really needy among the many callers at their door. To address this situation, a survey was done through the local parish council to try and identify the most vulnerable individuals. As a result of the findings of that survey, a list was drawn up that contained the names of a variety of individuals with different needs. A breakdown of the individuals showed that 40 per cent were bedridden, 30 per cent were physically disabled and 30 per cent were HIV-positive. It would be difficult to see how these people could become self-sufficient given their circumstances.

With the help of benefactors in Ireland, for example Project Zambia in Belfast, the Christian Brothers are able, on a monthly basis, to provide each of the poor individuals on the parish list with a food parcel containing some basic foodstuffs such as cooking oil, mealie-meal (maize flour), salt and sugar, as well as household essentials such as soap. Many of the people come to the house to collect their parcel of food each month or at least send somebody to collect on their behalf. Others who live at a distance from the parish have their parcels delivered to their homes at the end of each month by one of the brothers and a helper or two from the parish. Some young members of Project Zambia on a visit to Western Province were shocked to witness the levels of poverty in the villages. These young people were overwhelmed by the warmth and sincerity of the welcome they received from the people they met where the food programme operates. One young woman remarked that she 'never realised how poor some people could be'. The stories they heard of the hardships the people endured on a daily basis in these villages touched them deeply. Some of these poor people were victims of physical and sexual abuse in their own homes, abuses perpetrated quite often by a relative. Lack of education and understanding of the seriousness of these abuses kept the victims in an unending cycle of entrapment with little or no hope of being freed from this situation. Cultural norms dictated that many of the victims, both male and female, would never dare speak out against an older relative.

Giving to the poor in handfuls
The Mongu situation is in many respects akin to what prevailed in Waterford at the time of Blessed Edmund Rice. Poverty levels were extremely high back then and Edmund saw education as the key to helping people break out of the cycle of poverty. Education was to be the means of liberating the young people of that time, 'Educate them that they may be free,' we are told was a saying of Edmund's. When Edmund decided to give up his business interests and concentrate his efforts on helping the many poor street children in Waterford, it caused great shock among his business friends. Many tried to dissuade him from embarking on this new venture. He had no experience of teaching or being a formal educator and no doubt this was something that would have been pointed out to him by his business associates. However, he was a very determined man, and so nothing would stop him from beginning his project in a disused building in the city. When he established his first school at Mount Sion in Waterford, Edmund's keen, practical business sense led him to understand that young people just could not be expected to learn in a classroom situation if they were hungry or poorly clothed. So, he built a bakery and a tailoring shop right next to the new foundation. Edmund was a person with a heart for the poor. 'Give to the poor in handfuls' was a phrase he is said to have used over and over

when urging the early Christian Brothers to be mindful of those in need. In 1810 Edmund wrote: 'were we to know the merit and value of only going from one street to another to serve a neighbour for the love of God, we should prize it more than Gold or Silver.'[2]

Judgement, inequality and indifference

Pope Francis is a man with a real heart for the poor. He sees no problem in giving direct help to poor people, although there are those who at times frown upon charity work because, they believe, it keeps people dependent on donors rather than becoming self-reliant. Such critics would always maintain that people should be empowered to become self-sufficient and rely more on their own resources. But when one looks at the people who are part of the Mongu food programme, it's extremely difficult to see how these poor, physically challenged people could possibly become self-sufficient in the immediate or long-term future.

In an unprecedented gesture, on Sunday 17 November 2019, the third World Day of the Poor, Pope Francis celebrated Mass in St Peter's, Rome, in the company of hundreds of poor and homeless people. After the Mass Pope Francis hosted a meal in a large audience hall at the Vatican for all these poor people. In his homily that day Pope Francis remarked that, 'we go our way in haste, without worrying that gaps are increasing, that the greed of a few is adding to the poverty of many others.'[3] In his message on this occasion Pope Francis said:

> How many times do we see poor people rummaging through *garbage bins* to retrieve what others have discarded as superfluous, in the hope of finding something to live on or to wear! They themselves become part of a human garbage bin; they are

treated as refuse, without the slightest sense of guilt on the part of those who are complicit in this scandal. Frequently judged parasites on society, the poor are not even forgiven their poverty. Judgement is always around the corner. They are not allowed to be timid or discouraged; they are seen as a threat or simply useless, simply because they are poor.[4]

Elsewhere in his address Pope Francis quoted from psalm 10:1-10 where the Psalmist describes the condition of the poor and the arrogance of those who oppress them. The time in which the Psalmist wrote was a time when arrogant and ungodly people hounded the poor, seeking to take possession of even what little they had and to reduce them to bondage. Pope Francis noted that the situation in which the Psalmist wrote was not much different to what prevails in our world today: 'The economic crisis has not prevented large groups of people from accumulating fortunes that often appear all the more incongruous when, in the streets of our cities, we daily encounter great numbers of the poor who lack the basic necessities of life and are at times harassed and exploited.'[5]

It would seem that Pope Francis would endorse the work of the Mongu food programme when he stated that 'we Christians cannot stand with arms folded in indifference or thrown up in the air in helpless resignation. As believers we must *stretch out our hands*, as Jesus does with us'.[6]

Following a reminder of the command of Jesus to his disciples – 'You give them something to eat!' (Mk 6:37) – Pope Francis said that Christians are called to work for the elimination of the structural causes of poverty and to promote the integral development of the poor, as well as the small daily acts of solidarity in meeting the real needs which we encounter.[7]

The Mongu food programme endeavours to be faithful to this call by Pope Francis to reach out in faith and love to the most disadvantaged of the Lord's brothers and sisters and those who require most urgently the most basic assistance.

Conclusion

Obviously, no one person or organisation can overcome the enormous challenges presented by poverty in Western Province in Zambia or, indeed, around the world. The poor will always be with us. Back in 2005 there was a movement across Europe bringing aid and development agencies together whose motto was 'Make Poverty History'. Sadly, the overall situation doesn't seem to have changed much in the intervening years. What can we do to bring about a fairer distribution of the world's resources? Then, on climate change, for example, knowing that the poor always bear the brunt of hardship, are we even taking the basic call to reduce, reuse and recycle seriously enough? We know that all of these issues are connected. Again, some years ago we spoke of having an 'option for the poor'. People like Fr Peter McVerry SJ would say that we do not have an option for the poor, rather we have a duty towards the poor. If so, how well are we fulfilling our duty? Are we really reaching out our hands to the poor and giving in handfuls?

Reflection

- *John McCourt would face criticism from some for handing out food parcels and some basic necessities. Given the circumstances of the people of Western Province, what would you have done and what are you prepared to do now?*
- *How do you respond to the words of Edmund Rice when he says, without nuance or equivocation: 'Give to the poor in handfuls'? Do you believe that the question of world poverty*

is intimately connected with climate change, global injustice and inequality?
- What is your reading of the parable of the rich man and Lazarus in the Gospel of Luke? Do you find it disquieting? Do any of the words of Pope Francis, quoted by John McCourt, resonate or jar with you? Can you explain why?

Endnotes

1. Larry Elliott, 'World's 26 richest people own as much as poorest 50%, says Oxfam', *The Guardian*, 21 January 2019. Available at www.theguardian.com/business/2019/jan/21/world-26-richest-people-own-as-much-as-poorest-50-per-cent-oxfam-report; accessed 1 June 2022.

2. Letter from Edmund Rice to Bryan Bolger, 1810, in Desmond Rushe, *Edmund Rice: The Man and His Times*, Dublin: Gill and Macmillan, 1995, p. 76.

3. Pope Francis, Homily at Holy Mass on the World Day of the Poor, 17 November 2019. Available at https://www.vatican.va/content/francesco/en/homilies/2019/documents/papa-francesco_20191117_omelia-giornatamondiale-poveri.html; accessed 1 June 2022.

4. Pope Francis, Message for the third World Day of the Poor, 13 June 2019. Available at https://www.vatican.va/content/francesco/en/messages/poveri/documents/papa-francesco_20190613_messaggio-iii-giornatamondiale-poveri-2019.html; accessed 1 June 2022.

5. Ibid.

6. Pope Francis, Homily at Holy Mass on the World Day of the Poor, 18 November 2018. Available at https://www.vatican.va/content/francesco/en/homilies/2018/documents/papa-francesco_20181118_omelia-giornatamondiale-poveri.html; accessed 1 June 2022.

7. Cf. Pope Francis, *Evangelii Gaudium*, 118.

GOD COMES TO US IN DISGUISE

Peter McVerry

Learning about God from homeless people
I have worked with homeless people for the past forty years. I thought my job was somehow to reveal God to them. In fact, what happened was that they revealed God to me. They challenged me, my values and at least some of my prejudices. They changed my understanding of God, changed my relationship to God, and changed the way I read the gospel. And they made me angry – angry at how a society as wealthy as Ireland could tolerate a growing number of people living on the streets.

A young homeless man said to me one day, 'The very thought that there might be a God depresses me.' I was trying to understand what he meant – I'm used to young people telling me they don't believe in God, but this was going one step further. Eventually, I came to understand what he meant. He felt he was a bad person; he had broken all the commandments in the book (and a few more beside), so he thought that if God existed, God would be saying about him, 'There's a bad person; I couldn't possibly love him.' And if he died and went before God, God would say, 'Get away from me, you wretch. I want nothing to do with you.'

Now, I knew that young man very well. He had grown up in a home where he experienced a lot of violence, sexual abuse and extreme neglect. I could understand why he was angry and alienated. I thought to myself, 'If there is a God, he must have a warm place in his heart for this man who had suffered so horribly as a young, innocent child, and if he died and went before God, God must have a big welcome for him.' I could understand why he was unable to believe in such a God who loved him.

That homeless man challenged my understanding of God. I grew up believing in a God who had laid down the laws that he expected us to obey. If we obeyed those laws, God would love us and we would be rewarded with a place in heaven, but if we disobeyed those laws, then God would be angry with us and punish us. But working with homeless people, I came to believe in a God whose passion is not the observance of laws, but whose passion is compassion; a God who cares about our pain and our suffering; a God who understands why we behave so badly at times and makes excuses for us; a God who forgives us again and again.

Jesus, Pope Francis and the God of compassion
Jesus was constantly in the company of the poor, the sick, the sinners and the rejected. Everywhere he went, huge crowds turned out to listen to him – five thousand on at least one occasion. They didn't come to listen to Jesus laying down laws and preaching a God who will judge them by how they observe those laws, as their own religious authorities preached. No, they came to listen to Jesus talking about a God of compassion, who cared about their suffering, their poverty and their marginalisation. They listened to Jesus talk about the greed, the inequality, the accumulation of wealth and the abuse of power in the kingdom of Herod that was making their lives a misery, and how this was an affront to the God of compassion.[1] They came to listen to Jesus talking about a new kingdom

that was coming, over which the God of compassion will rule, where greed will be replaced by the caring and sharing of the community, and those who are rejected and excluded will be welcomed, valued and respected. But others came, listened, and went away to plot 'how to destroy him' (Mk 3:6). These were the religious leaders who passionately believed, in good conscience, that Jesus was undermining the faith of the people, and therefore inviting the anger of God to descend upon the people, by failing to emphasise the importance of observing the law and censure those who do not keep it.

Today people do not come to listen to Pope Francis laying down laws and telling people what they must do and what they must not do. No, they come in their millions – six million in Manila! – to listen to Pope Francis because everything he says and does reveals a God of compassion; a God who cares about the suffering of the poor, migrants, refugees, prisoners and homeless people. They listen to Francis talking about the greed, the inequality, the accumulation of wealth and the abuse of power in our world today that is keeping many in extreme poverty and misery, and how this is an affront to the God of compassion.[2] They listen to Francis hoping for a new world in which the rich will share with the poor, the economy will serve everyone and not just a privileged few, and those who rule will promote the common good and not their own self-interest. But, as in the time of Jesus, some religious leaders today believe that Pope Francis is undermining the faith of the people, and leading the Church astray, by failing to emphasise the importance of observing the law and of censuring those who do not keep it. They are not plotting how to destroy him. Instead, they are praying that Pope Francis will have a happy death – and soon! Others – usually the rich and the powerful – listen to him talking about a more just world and dismiss him as a 'Marxist'.

Does it matter if our God is a God whose passion is the observance of the law or a God whose passion is compassion? Yes, it makes all the difference. We have been given our faith, not just as a personal gift, to be kept to ourselves, to console us in time of difficulty, to absolve us when we sin and affirm us when we live good lives. We are a missionary Church. We are given our faith to share it with others, to reveal God to others. How do we reveal to others a God of the law? Why, by affirming the law without hesitation, welcoming those who keep it and censuring those who do not. But we cannot reveal a God of compassion from the pulpit. We can only reveal a God of compassion by being the compassion of God to others. A spirituality based on a God of the law has, as its primary focus, the state of our soul. A spirituality based on a God of compassion reminds us that the state of our soul is intrinsically linked to the state of our neighbour. As the American physician and humanitarian Paul Farmer famously stated, 'If I am hungry, that is a material problem; if someone else is hungry, that is a spiritual problem.'

A world in need of transformation and redemption

Every Christmas, some homeless people want to give me a little gift. But they don't know what to give me. So they give me a shirt. I could open a shop with all the shirts I've got. Of course, it would be impolite to ask them to show me a receipt! But one Christmas a homeless man gave me a watch. It just so happened that my watch had broken, although he was unaware of that, and so it was a gift I really needed. Working with homeless people and listening to their stories of tragic childhoods and broken relationships, I came to realise how blessed I have been by God. So I want to give God a gift in gratitude. But what gift can I give God? God needs nothing and, anyway, everything I have has already been given to me by God. But if God needs nothing, the children of God have many needs. By reaching out to the needs of God's children, I am giving God a gift that God really wants.

Every parent's desire is that their children live happy, healthy and fulfilling lives. Every human being without exception is God's beloved child. God's deepest desire, too, is that all his children live happy, healthy and fulfilling lives. But this world we live in today is one where one billion people go to bed hungry every night, where children die from malnutrition, a lack of medicines or clean drinking water, where war destroys millions of lives, where refugees find no welcome anywhere, where the poor are rejected and marginalised even in wealthy countries. The world that we live in today is not the world that God desires. We Christians are called to be people who are angry – angry at the way things are, angry with all that limits or diminishes human beings, angry at all that denies the dignity of each child of God. Christians are meant to be 'protesters' – protesting against the chronic violence and injustice that blight the lives of so many of God's children. Christians see in every situation of suffering something unacceptable, something outrageous, something to be angry about. Christians are meant to be revolutionaries – people who look at the world as it is and say, 'This is not the way things are meant to be.' We are called to change the way the world today is, to the way the world tomorrow should be. Jesus sought to change the way things were. He railed against the poverty of the majority of people by identifying himself with those in need: 'I was hungry and you gave me food' (Mt 25:35). He objected to his society's exclusion of certain people, by eating 'with tax collectors and sinners' (Lk 5:30). He spent his whole public life training twelve people to be agents of change. Jesus, too, was angry. He was angry when he threw the buyers and sellers out of the temple; he was angry when the religious leaders would not allow him to cure a sick person on the Sabbath because it was against the law; he was angry when he called the Pharisees 'hypocrites'.

We are often told that anger is a sin, to be confessed, that we Christians should be cultivating inner peace, serenity and acceptance. But while anger can often be an emotion which people fail to control and which explodes destructively, causing pain and hurt, nevertheless, we Christians are meant to be angry people. Anger and love are two sides of the same coin: we cannot love someone who is suffering unnecessarily without being angry at what is causing their suffering. We Christians should be angry at children having to wait months, often in pain, for necessary surgery; angry at the growing tide of homeless adults and children while houses remain empty and boarded up; angry at families being evicted by banks who seek the maximum sale price; angry that women fleeing domestic violence have to be turned away from refuges because they are full; angry that children come into school hungry; angry that one in five children live in households below the poverty line; angry that people with untreated mental health problems end up in prison. We Christians should be angry at the gross inequalities created by a global economic system which, while excluding millions of people, enriches a tiny number beyond precedent, who parade their wealth before the eyes of those excluded and in poverty. We live in a world gone wrong, where human bodies and hearts are crushed daily, a world that once crucified the Son of God and continues today to crucify the sons and daughters of God. The prophets of old denounced the way things were. We Christians today are called to denounce the way things are.

Called to repent: called to be the 'salt of the earth'
The peace promised by Jesus does not come from accepting the world as it is, but from the hope for what is promised for the future. The Christian community was established by Jesus in order to show a broken world how to live as the new creation. The Christian community, by the way we live, love, care and share with each other, is called to say no to our world as it is, to say yes to the world as it should be, over which God can happily reign. We are called to be the 'light of the world,' showing the world how people should live together, caring and sharing, loving and respecting everyone. We are called to be the 'salt of the earth', showing the world the meaning of life lived together in love. But if we stop caring and sharing, loving and respecting everyone, then 'the salt has lost its taste' and 'is no longer good for anything but is thrown out and trampled under foot' (Mt 5:13). Jesus constantly asked people to 'repent.' The word 'repent' didn't just mean 'be sorry for your sins'. It's meaning could also be translated as 'turn around', a U-turn in the way people live, a total change of lifestyle. People were part of a system with which they were comfortable, and Jesus called them to 'turn around' and move out of their comfort zones. 'Repent' meant dying to our rights ('it is mine, I can do what I want with it') so that others might have their rights. Jesus said to his disciples:

> You have heard that it was said, 'An eye for an eye and a tooth for a tooth.' But I say to you, Do not resist an evildoer. But if anyone strikes you on the right cheek, turn the other also, and if anyone wants to sue you and take your coat, give him your cloak as well, and if anyone forces you to go one mile, go also the second mile. Give to everyone who begs from you,

and do not refuse anyone who wants to borrow from you. (Mt 5:38-42)

In today's world, our western culture has exalted individualism above the common good. The gospel, however, exalts the common good above individualism. Today 'repentance' means challenging this culture we live in, putting solidarity at the centre of our spirituality, a modern-day U-turn.

Encountering God in disguise

God comes to us in disguise. At Christmas, we believe that the all-powerful God came amongst us as a poor, vulnerable, dependent child. At Easter, we believe that the convicted criminal hanging on the cross is, in fact, the all-loving Son of God. Today God comes among us in the poor, the homeless, the lonely, the sick, refugees, prisoners, those whom we prefer to keep at arm's length. The God of compassion identifies with those who are unwanted and ignored. In them, we encounter God:

> 'I was hungry and you gave me food, I was thirsty and you gave me something to drink, I was a stranger and you welcomed me, I was naked and you gave me clothing, I was sick and you took care of me, I was in prison and you visited me.' Then the righteous will answer him, 'Lord, when was it that we saw you hungry and gave you food, or thirsty and gave you something to drink? And when was it that we saw you a stranger and welcomed you, or naked and gave you clothing? And when was it that we saw you sick or in prison and visited you?' And the king will answer them, 'Truly I tell you, just as you did it to one of the least of these who are members of my family, you did it to me. (Mt 25:35-45)

God Comes to Us in Disguise

The gospel is not just about bringing God's love to the poor and the unwanted. They also bring God's love to us. Indeed, salvation comes to us only from the poor. The poor and the unwanted offer us the greatest gift that anyone can offer us: they invite us, in their need, to open our hearts to include them in our love. If we open our hearts to include them in our love, then we become more loving persons and therefore we become more like God. No greater gift can anyone offer us than the gift of becoming more like God. If, then, we fail to reach out to those who are unwanted and ignored, we fail not only them, but ourselves, for we reject their invitation to grow in love. In rejecting this invitation, we show ourselves to be not yet ready for the kingdom of God. Accepting the invitation of the unwanted and ignored is not an invitation to be charitable; it is an invitation to be just. A world where some are poor and marginalised, in the midst of wealth, is an unjust world, a contradiction to the world desired by God. It cannot be, or become, the kingdom of God while such injustice remains. Again, Paul Farmer tells us: 'The idea that some lives matter less is the root of all that is wrong with the world.' Hence, to build the kingdom of God we must remedy the injustices that exist. It is in our efforts to build a more just world that we enter the kingdom of God.

I got a phone call one Christmas morning from a homeless man, who was already pretty drunk. He said, 'Happy Christmas, Peter.' I replied, 'Happy Christmas to you too.' Then he asked, 'What did you get for Christmas?' Now, presuming that he had got nothing for Christmas, and not wanting him to feel that he was the only one who had got nothing, I said, 'I got nothing for Christmas. How about you? I presume you got nothing either.' He thought for a moment and then said, 'No, God gave me a present this Christmas. God gave me you.' And in that comment, that drunken homeless man summed up the gospel better than any professional theologian.

Jesus came 'to bring good news to the poor' (Lk 4:18). What is that good news? It is you and I. And if you and I are not the good news to the poor, then the poor have no good news.

Reflection
- *When we see those who are homeless, who are begging on the streets, people with mental health issues, people suffering from addiction or poverty we sometimes are moved to pity. These are, surely, unfortunate people who need our help. It is we – good Christians – who must bring God's love to them. Yet when Peter McVerry encounters the poor and marginalised, he sees something different altogether. He sees God in them and understands that it is us who need them as it is only through 'the least of these' that we meet God.*
- *When we encounter the homeless and the poor and those begging on our streets do we see them as poor people to be pitied and in need of our help – or even avoided? Or do we – like Fr Peter McVerry today or Edmund Rice when looking out the window in Waterford more than two centuries ago – see them as God's children and God himself?*
- *Do we only seek to encounter God in the tabernacle and not recognise him in the beggar we meet on the street every day?*
- *Do we even recognise our own spiritual poverty and our need to be saved?*

Endnotes

1   See, for example, Lk 12:13-21; Lk 16:19-31.
2   See Pope Francis, *Evangelii Gaudium*, 53, 205.

BREAKING DOWN RACIAL AND ETHNIC BARRIERS TO SPIRITUAL DIRECTION

Don Bisson

Social, cultural and spiritual context of spiritual direction

As I write this, hundreds of thousands have died from Covid-19 and infections are now into the millions. The world is struggling to come to grips with the pandemic sweeping across the developed world and into the barrios of the poorest countries of the southern hemisphere. Edmund Rice, the founder of the Christian Brothers, and Marcellin Champagnat, the founder of the Marist Brothers, both would have noticed the inadequate responses to the poor and marginalised in our society. Why are poor neighbourhoods and countries being hit harder than others? Why are their death rates higher than in other parts of cities and nations? Who is meeting the physical, emotional, pastoral, social and spiritual needs of these communities and what does this have to do with spiritual direction?

Well, the ministry of spiritual direction clearly does not exist in a vacuum cut off from the social and cultural context of a society. Those in the ministry live within this world experience and, like all parts of the society, are being transformed by the pandemic. Over the past ten weeks I have been in lockdown in the Bronx in New York City, one of the hardest hit areas, with a hospital system on the brink of disaster. For over a month, as the urban noises silenced around us, all we heard day and night were the ambulances rushing to a nearby hospital at the apex of the disaster. Our high school for boys, which has a 95 per cent minority enrolment, has closed. Our parish, made up of African Americans, Latinx and new immigrants from the Caribbean and Africa, has shuttered until further notice. Only the food pantry sponsored by the parish has boomed, with a 300 per cent increase as thousands have lost their jobs or found themselves ill.

We are seeing similar situations around the world, equally blatant in their cultural context. Those most likely to get the disease are not the privileged who can work safely from home and have distance between each other. The front-line individuals of society, the bus drivers and hospital workers, who keep society functioning, are at greater risk of getting Covid-19. African Americans, Native Americans and other minorities have a greater history of poor or non-existent healthcare and preventative medicine and a higher risk of diseases such as high blood pressure, diabetes and obesity. They have two to three times the possibility of acquiring Covid-19 and of dying from it. The immigrants who pick our food and deliver our packages are tools to keep the economy going; the term used by economists is 'human stock', the necessary but dispensable bottom that keeps our inflated life style afloat – until we can find machinery to replace them. The pandemic lightens the darkness beneath our structures and has put the spotlight on income disparity around the world. One of the darkest evils, almost banal now in its expression, is the absolute absence of empathy for others. This is one of the greatest spiritual scandals of a society, in which those suffering are invariably written off and viewed as weak, complaining and not believable.

Children are taken away from Latinx parents at the United States border under horrible circumstances. An African-American man gasping for air is not believed by the police and is left to die. A young, innocent black jogger is immediately 'identified' as a runaway thief and summarily killed in the streets, without any human dignity. Cold-blooded murder reigns. Not only does the system solely serve those who can afford the best, but there exists also a culture of blaming the victims for being unhealthy, not knowing their rights and not being informed.

The shocking thing is, and I have known this for a long time, the inequality actually exists in the spiritual realm as well. I have been involved in this ministry for forty years. I was at the first Spiritual Directors International (SDI) meeting in Burlingame, California, and have helped with the formation of spiritual directors throughout the world. As a Marist Brother, I have been privileged to live in multi-cultural settings for over twenty years in New York, Chicago and Oakland. I have had the experience of listening to men and women of different cultures, backgrounds and struggles. It has been one of the deepest joys of my life. This reality also causes me deep suffering and fuels my anger at the historical injustices that are repeated in our society. We need a revolution of the heart, as Dorothy Day so aptly put it. Instead, however, we continue to reinforce racism, misogyny and a puritan ethic that defines one's human value by economic success. My inner-city experiences continue to reinforce the lenses through which I view reality.

When I left Oakland to work at Mercy Center in Burlingame, a distance of less than twenty miles, I entered a whole different world. I lived with survivors' guilt. I went through a period of healing from some symptoms of PTSD and a sense of powerlessness to help the loved ones I left behind. I have always tried to connect with the formation of directors. I sought to assist those who did not have access to spiritual direction, or to the retreats that I fostered in the inner city. I saw an apartheid of spirituality that has now blossomed. Spirituality centres of every kind offer therapy, holistic healthcare, yoga, spiritual counselling, etc., and are found in well-off, middle-class, suburban communities rather than in the inner city.

There is even arrogance around being spiritual and not religious and outright dismissal of the idea that one can be both spiritual and religious. A new duality has been created. So, who has access to spiritual direction in our society? With the growing split between religion and spirituality, it is far less available in church than outside of church structures. Religious structures are not addressing the deep spiritual needs of congregations but are either advocating clerical piety or collective, devotional expressions from the past. Too many churches are either ignorant of, or adverse to, such lay movements as centring prayer or spiritual direction. The pandemic may give us an opportunity to assess and change this reality.

Spiritual direction ministry challenges
Since the restoration of spiritual direction, there has been an evolution that, in many ways, has opened the doors for a whole generation of seekers to move forward on their spiritual journey. However, every movement can have a counter movement. It is difficult for a person, and especially a society, to hold the tension of seeming opposites for a creative solution. With my Jungian background, I am always interested in the shadow we create by rejection of one

end of the spectrum. Spiritual direction was held captive in clerical systems identified with the confessional in the Catholic Church and was not practiced at all in many other denominations and traditions, so a liberation was necessary. This has created a powerful counter influence. If an extreme, one-sided tendency begins to dominate conscious life, in time an equally powerful counter position is built up in the psyche and in society. This fragmentation is capable of producing horrible consequences in our politics and in religion. Young priests, for example, commit to undo the 'excesses' of Vatican II by a regression to a less than idealised past. Political parties, no longer in conversation with one another, go from one extreme to another in election pledges and policy statements. One party promises to undo everything the earlier party had accomplished. One pastor undoes all the elements from the previous pastor as he takes over. This lack of wholeness causes us to respond to things in knee-jerk reactions, wasting time and energy and collectively not growing in consciousness.

Throughout the world there are many examples of spiritual direction being done with folks on the margins. However, I believe the culture of spiritual direction has moved more and more towards an elite form of self-help and is not generally available to ordinary folks, much less to those on the margins. I have also noticed some disturbing trends in the culture of spiritual direction that I wish to highlight. These trends not only isolate spiritual direction from most; one has to ask if we have entirely lost our way. Many of these themes do not spark a response from cultures less educated, with multi-faith sensitivity or psychological sophistication. Here are some of my concerns for spiritual direction. They are also some of the reasons why those who might benefit the most from spiritual direction are, in fact, those who are less likely to have it made available to them:

1. There has been a great deal of influence in recent years by the New Age movement. This multi-billion-dollar business around the world can act as a substitute for authentic spirituality. When one goes to a bookshop, the dual categories of New Age and spirituality often coexist in the same space. There is equal attention to Teresa of Ávila and a New Age teacher. This smorgasbord approach leaves seekers who may be without sufficient background knowledge open to charlatans and magical thinking.
2. The idealism around spirituality suggests that nearly everything, without discretion, if it is called spiritual, is actually helpful. This lends itself to the possible emergence of charlatans who solely seek the same power, money and sensuality that can often be found in politics and religion.
3. In many of these New Age approaches to spirituality there is a marked absence of real community. Seekers find themselves on a solitary esoteric path and do not have the structures for common prayer and ritual. Rituals are taken outside of a culture and imaged and used for personal enrichment. Can yoga be misused? Can the rites of letting go of ego actually be used to mollify the ego against growth beyond itself? Can Native American and indigenous rituals be used by upper-middle-class persons seeking a spiritual high? Can we idealise a culture without critiquing its inherent injustices and the suffering it may cause?
4. Psychology has had a positive influence on spiritual direction. My doctoral studies were in the area of Jungian analytical psychology and the transformational experience in spiritual direction. I am deeply convinced that the use of material from the unconscious can lead to spiritual growth and a more intense relationship with God. However, I also believe that the rise of professionalisation

in this ministry takes it in a direction away from community. The therapeutic model of the office with all its stipulations and boundaries does not fit spiritual direction in a faith community. Financially, it takes the charism and quantifies its value. This is worrisome for me; it tends to distance people from the ministry and focus too much on problem-solving and personal growth rather than an authentic relationship with God.

5. Spiritual direction is first and foremost a gift from the Spirit. Much of the formation of spiritual directors is the discernment of the call and to whom are they called to serve. A major component of our formation programme in Linwood Spiritual Center is listening to the voice of God to serve those who have the greatest need. Our interns have crossed over into direction in men's and women's prisons, working with the elderly in homes, alcoholic recovery centres, etc. This focus on who are we being called to serve is a critical need in all programmes.

A practical response to the cultural and spiritual challenges

Spiritual direction needs to go beyond some of these evolutionary choices. I have been extremely blessed in ministry. A major synchronistic event took place recently that opened a whole new focus of spiritual direction for the near future. An opportunity for legacy and generativity for my last stage in life has been afforded to me. Within a three-week period, I was able to form a team and find finances and floor space to run an inner-city programme for forming spiritual directors from the African American, Latinx and immigrant Asian community. Let it be said that the Spirit was moving and the chemistry of all this came together mysteriously.

The Marist Brothers Formation Programme was born in the Bronx and has even survived the pandemic through mentoring, spiritual direction and readings by way of Zoom. It is a two-year programme of five weekends. The first year focuses on foundational topics, i.e. discernment, prayer, images of God, and religious experiences. The second year primarily focuses on providing supervision and refining the skills necessary for each intern to grow in their ministry. Through financial support we were able to invite educated, mature leaders of different communities to be our first intern group without the limitations of money being a problem. These men and women of faith and commitment come from educational, religious, health, social work and non-profit organisational backgrounds. The programme aims to empower each and every one of them to leadership in spiritual direction within those communities.

Communities of faith greatly benefit through listening deeply to their elders and other wise women and men committed to leading spiritual lives. All of the interns come with rich and varied multi-cultural experiences of support and love. Community is not an option, it is a necessity. God lives and breathes in the interaction of faith-filled lovers of God. The course offers people from different cultures and backgrounds the opportunity to articulate their unique experience of God, in their own language, and to listen deeply to and be enriched by the experiences of others. Attending our parish liturgy, a pastor from Nigeria invited us to stand and be recognised as a charism being formed by and for the community. Parishes are opening up their doors to spiritual direction in Manhattan, South Bronx and North Bronx. The need is here, and the presence of God is so real and tangible. Here are some immediate learnings:

1. This training underscores certain truths. We are radically similar in our common human condition and our deepest desire for love and union with God is in the core of our

souls. We cannot be separated from God; we are all manifestations of the Divine among us.
2. We are also blessed and broken. No one escapes the story of life and suffering. We are all in the paschal mystery of suffering, death and resurrection.
3. We are all invited on the journey to maturity and individuation. God is creating and recreating us from our depths. The body and spirit are either at war or are being gradually integrated as a whole.
4. Though radical similar, we are also radically different. The need to listen to stories with open hearts and minds to discover the beauty of another's life without judging is a powerful moment. The mystery of the other is profoundly felt with compassion and joy and sorrow.
5. Uniquely, we are aware of social sins and injustices, prejudices and hurdles from the outer world. We also recognise the introjection and lies coming from a racist society that influences our self-identity and limits our gifts. This shadow is not only personal but takes on many forms of bigotry and evil. How does one heal from the evil done generationally? This is an important element in this mode of spiritual direction.

Conclusion

Through word of mouth, the Marist Brothers fund now helps programmes in the central valley in California with directors for migrant workers. Spanish speakers in Sacramento will be trained with assistance from the Mercy Sisters. A potential project in Appalachia for rural poor, with a Catholic Workers community, is in the planning stage. It will bring spiritual direction to God's rural poor people. God seems to desire this ministry to grow. I see a three-pronged approach: first, to make spiritual direction available to those who have been marginalised and until now have not had the opportunity to receive this ministry; second, to provide for the formation of minorities to do direction in their communities of faith; and third, to make provision for handing on the baton for the training of formators from these communities so as to extend the ministry further. The spiritual apartheid must end. I believe both Edmund Rice and Marcellin Champagnat would be pleased with these attempts to assist all on the journey to God through the ministry of spiritual direction. The pandemic now fosters action. The revelation of the truth of our world needs to be addressed in a loving revolution of solidarity and inter-dependence. The duality of spirituality and religion can be bridged with maturity and strength. The extension of leadership in spiritual direction ministry, to those who have traditionally not had it as an option, is a small way of seeing the reign of God blossom and grow in our midst.

Reflection
- *The pandemic has shown us clearly that it is low-paid workers who keep our society functioning. Therefore, they are among those at greatest risk and yet their communities have benefited least from the healthcare services. Is injustice systemic in our societies?*
- *What do you think of Don's assertion that a spiritual apartheid is rampant in our world? Are you disturbed, as he is, by aspects of the New Age movement, by spiritual elitism, by the strong emphasis on the shadow side of religion and by the absence of real community?*
- *What do you think of his inner-city programme for the training of people for leadership in spiritual direction and the learnings that already seem to be evident? What potential has such a programme into the future? Is such training needed in your local church?*

NEW PATHS FOR THE CHURCH AND FOR INTEGRAL ECOLOGY: A CHALLENGE FOR THE UNIVERSAL CHURCH

Sheila Curran

Introduction

A key issue affecting the poor all over the world today is environmental destruction. This topic was a particular focus of the special assembly of the synod of bishops for the Pan-Amazon region on the theme 'Amazonia: New Paths for the Church and for Integral Ecology' and Pope Francis' apostolic exhortation *Querida Amazonia*. Today the Christian Brothers have members ministering in the Pan-Amazon region. The Amazon region is commonly called the 'lungs of the world', a place of tremendous biodiversity, which contains 20 per cent of the world's unfrozen water. The region is under threat and our entire planet is affected by what is happening in there. Today more than ever we are called to become aware of our duties towards our planet and to the listen to indigenous communities who have been deemed 'insignificant' throughout the course of history. It is always the poor who suffer most. The significance and role of the Pan-Amazon region in terms of the ecological well-being of the planet is undisputed and it has been scientifically proven that the whole world is in danger if this region is destroyed. I believe the two documents stemming from the synod of bishops offer guidance as to how we might begin to respond to the challenge to create 'new paths for the Church and integral ecology'.

The special assembly of the synod of bishops for the Pan-Amazon region

This historic event did not take place, unfortunately, in the Amazon Region but in Rome from 6 to 27 October in 2019. While the composition of the synod was a disappointment to many, it is important to note that the input of at least ninety thousand Catholics from nine countries sharing the Pan-Amazonian region (Peru, Ecuador, Colombia, Venezuela, Guyana, French Guyana, Surinam, Brazil and Bolivia) were included in the preparatory document which was used throughout the synod. This was the first time in the history of the Church that the Amazon region was the *locus theologicus* and the indigenous people were being consulted on how the Church can accompany them today. In attendance were 185 synod fathers along with 16 representatives of different Amazonian indigenous communities and 34 women as auditors or experts, though they had no voting rights. It is interesting to note that one lay religious brother had been granted voting rights at the synod but sadly the same right was not extended to any woman, even though there were twenty religious sisters at the synod who had the same canonical status as the brother. This is the third consecutive synod of bishops in which a religious brother was counted among the members and allowed to vote but no women religious nor any member of the indigenous representatives, despite the richness of their experience, were given voting rights.

In his post-synodal exhortation *Querida Amazonia* (QA),[1] Pope Francis officially presents the final document of the synod: *The Amazon: New Paths for the Church and for an Integral Ecology*.[2] He acknowledges that the document 'profited from the participation of many who know better than myself or the Roman Curia the problems and issues of the Amazon region, since they live there, they experience its suffering and they live it passionately' (*QA* 3). He prays that the 'entire Church will be enriched and challenged by the work of the synodal assembly' (*QA* 4). In the light of this whole synodal process, a clear and new hermeneutic is proposed between the final document of the synod and the apostolic exhortation. Pope Francis is very clear in saying that the exhortation does not replace the final document of the synod (*QA* 2), but rather assumes it (*QA* 3) and invites us to read it and apply it (*QA* 3–4). I understand that this is the first time in the universal magisterium that a final document of a regional synod and the papal magisterium that follows it are given equal status. It is important to note that the special synod's conclusions transcend the ecclesial-Amazonian region as similar issues are experienced across our globe.[3]

The Amazon: New Paths for the Church and for an Integral Ecology

The final document, consisting of five chapters and 120 paragraphs, was approved with the necessary two-thirds majority. One of the key messages from the final document can be summed up in the word 'conversion'. Each chapter looks at conversion under the following areas: integral, pastoral, cultural, ecological and synodal.

To begin the process of conversion we must acknowledge the complicity of the Church during the colonisation of the Americas. The document reminds us that 'the proclamation of Christ often took place in collusion with the powers that exploited the resources and oppressed the local populations'.

The Church has a 'historic opportunity to distance herself' from 'the new colonising powers, by listening to the Amazonian peoples and acting in a transparent and prophetic manner' (15). In order to do this, we need to:

> make clear where we stand, whose side we are on, what perspective we assume, how the political and ethical dimension of our word of faith and life are transmitted. For this reason: a) we denounce the violation of human rights and extractive destruction; b) we embrace and support campaigns of divestment from extractive companies responsible for the socio-ecological damage of the Amazon, starting with our own Church institutions and also in alliance with other churches. (70)

Chapter 3 is dedicated to 'new paths of cultural conversion'. To achieve cultural conversion we need to promote intercultural dialogue by learning from and listening to the indigenous people and promoting a Church with an 'Amazonian face' (86). This is a challenge. During the synod, wooden statues of a pregnant Amazonian woman, symbols of the *Pachamama* (a goddess revered by the indigenous peoples of the Andes, though now often associated with the Virgin Mary), were used as part of a display in the Church of Santa Maria in Traspontina, which is located near the Vatican City. They were stolen and thrown into the Tiber river – an act based on the claim that they were idolatrous. Pope Francis, in his role as bishop of Rome, apologised and asked forgiveness of the Amazonian bishops and tribal leaders. He acknowledged that these symbols were placed in the church 'without any intention of idolatry'.[4] Therefore, the need for theological research and education based on the identity and culture of the Amazonian region is highlighted (57–9). We are being called to inculturate our liturgies and representations of the divine.

In keeping with the theme of conversion, the final document calls on us to acknowledge our 'ecological sin' It states that ecological sin is 'an action or an omission against God, against one's neighbour, the community and the environment' (82), calling on us to look for ways in which we can repay our ecological debt, emphasising the urgent need to reduce emissions of carbon dioxide and other gases related to climate change.

Chapter 5 of the document explores new ways of synodal conversion, recognising the need to overcome clericalism and a pastoral approach based on a culture of listening and dialogue:

> In order to walk together, the Church today needs a conversion to the synodal experience. It needs to strengthen a culture of dialogue, reciprocal listening, spiritual discernment, consensus and communion in order to find areas and ways of joint decision-making and to respond to pastoral challenges. (88)

The pastoral challenges, particularly, access to Eucharist in the remote areas of the Amazon are acknowledged and the issues of *viri probati*, married clergy and the need for an Amazonian Rite were debated. After much discussion, paragraph 111, which addressed these topics, got over two-thirds of the votes at 128 votes in favour, though it also attracted the largest number of negative votes with forty-one voting against. The issues have been left open. Space is also given to the role of women, the need for women's voices to be heard and for women participate in the decision-making, along with recognition for women who are leaders within communities (100–103). The issue of women deacons was also debated. The Synod also called on all of us to recognise what constitutes 'good living, *bien vivir*', which is described as:

> a matter of living in harmony with oneself, with nature, with human beings and with the Supreme Being, since there is intercommunication throughout the cosmos; here there are neither exclusions nor those who exclude, and here a full life for all can be projected. (9)

What I have outlined here is only a flavour of what is contained in this document. Normally, the final synodal document has no teaching or binding authority on its own. This time, Pope Francis launched the final document of the Amazon synod along with his own exhortation, which, as I said earlier, is quite remarkable. The final document reflects the voice of the people of the Amazon and therefore needs to be read in its entirety.

Pope Francis' exhortation *Querida Amazonia*

Querida Amazonia, like *Laudato Si'* before it, is addressed to 'the people of God and to *all* people of good will' (emphasis added). It is Pope Francis' personal response to the synod experience. The exhortation forms a single unit with the preparatory and final documents.

The exhortation expresses affection for those who are made poor, those who are in some way despised by the technocratic society in which we live and who suffer the consequences of this same system that puts profit above the dignity of persons, cultures and our 'common home'. The document analyses all the suffering that has been inflicted on the indigenous people and the destruction of the natural environment in the region. It calls us to advance human and ecological integration that allows for a truly human life, without oppression and injustice. Pope Francis speaks of four great dreams for the Amazon region (social, cultural, ecological and ecclesial), and develops in detail each of these dreams. He asks us to be on the side of the Amazonian people, to hear their pleas but to do so in a spirit of encounter and dialogue, beginning by listening to the poor (*QA* 26). Pope Francis acknowledges the destructive role of the Church and reiterates his apology 'not only for the offenses of the Church herself, but for crimes committed against the native peoples during the so-called conquest of America' (*QA* 19). He cautions us against new forms of colonisation and corruption, asking us to listen to, and journey with, the indigenous peoples so that we can learn to *contemplate* the Amazon region, 'love it, not simply use it', 'feel intimately a part of it and not only defend it', so that the Amazon region will 'once more become like a mother to us' (*QA* 55). He calls us all to examine and change our consumeristic lifestyle and 'culture of waste' by reflecting on the consequences that our decisions have on the environment (*QA* 58). In addressing the area of inculturation, he challenges us to 'imagine a holiness with Amazonian features, called to challenge the universal Church' (*QA* 77).

One of the challenges of ministry in the Amazon region, is the access to the Eucharist and other sacraments. With respect to women deacons and married priests, Pope Francis' response is inadequate, even though he has left the question open. These requests still stand in the final document. The Pope also calls for more opportunities for women to access 'positions, including ecclesial services' but not Holy Orders. These ecclesial services he envisions 'would entail stability, public recognition and a commission from the bishop'. This would also 'allow women to have a real and effective impact on the organisation, the most important decisions and the direction of communities, while continuing to do so in a way that reflects their womanhood' (*QA* 103). Pope Francis' exhortation is offered in a spirit of 'dialogue and discernment' (*QA* 2). We are being invited into that process.

Conclusion
The indigenous people from the Pan-Amazon region have been trying to tell us for centuries that that everything is interconnected. They do not have a vision of God that separates them from the world, dominating and ruling over the world from a distance. They understand the divine as an integral part of the universe. They keep telling us that we cannot continue to exploit Mother Earth and live well. They know that the loss of biodiversity and climate change will bring us many humanitarian catastrophes of biblical proportions. Therefore, we cannot continue to ignore their voices. The Covid-19 pandemic has forced us to consider what really counts, life or material goods? Many people from the Amazon region have been defending life by exposing with clarity the corruption of political, economic and social systems, illustrating how they prioritise profit over human life, community and our earth. People have suffered and many lost their lives denouncing violations of human rights and standing up to powerful extractive industries.[5] If we as Church are to be prophetic and stand in solidarity with the poor and the people from the Amazon region, we have to pray for the courage to continue to denounce human rights violations and confront the exploitation of companies involved in the extractive industries as well as demanding a UN global treaty on business and human rights.[6] We have to begin to illustrate what matters and what does not matter.

The people from the Pan-Amazon region are calling on the Church to change its own environment, raising serious questions on inculturation and eucharistic celebrations. As someone who believes in the need for systemic change within our Church, I found Pope Francis' response to the question of married clergy and the role of women very disappointing. These questions will not go away. Catholic women can and should take on a greater role in Church decisions. Patriarchy and clericalism within the Church are preventing women from doing so. Pope Francis has been openly and repeatedly critical of clericalism as 'an illness in the Church' calling it 'our ugliest perversion' and 'the culture that enables abuse and insists on hiding it'.[7] Women are often at the forefront of environmental change and defending human rights. They are also among the poor and marginalised to whom Pope Francis calls us to listen. The final document of the synod still stands, which means that these questions are now in the hands of the bishops of the Amazon region and the Latin American Church. Base Christian communities, which are lay lead, were affirmed as 'experiences of synodality' (QA 94). Perhaps they will take the prophetic and creative step putting synodality into practice by giving a place to all the baptised to discern the way forward and 'find ways not yet even imagined' (QA 104). We cannot put 'new wine into old wineskins'. The indigenous people were re-echoing the call from Vatican II for the Church to open its windows to world, to engage with them, to change its structures to form new, living ways that reflect the interconnectedness of all of life. At the end of the day we are 'united by the struggle for peace and justice' (QA 109). Pope Francis asks, 'How can we not struggle together? How can we not pray and work together, side by side, to defend the poor of the Amazon region, to show the sacred countenance of the Lord, and to care for God's creation?' (QA 110).

The synod on the Amazon is setting out 'new paths for the Church and for an integral ecology' and calling on us to expand our worldview. This is only the beginning, as Pope Francis insists; synodality is an ongoing process. We are now all invited by Pope Francis to 'sit around the common table, a place of conversation and of shared hopes. In this way our differences, which could seem like a banner or a wall, can become a bridge' (*QA* 37). The Covid-19 pandemic, as an unprecedented crisis, illustrates our interdependence with one another and with our common home. The invitation from the Amazonian people presents us with an immediate pathway to change our lives and our theological thinking. It is imperative that we respond to this challenge to ensure that another world is possible.

Reflection:
- *What stays with you after reading this chapter? What troubles you? What gives you hope?*
- *The Church participated in the colonisation of the Americas and in the great wrongs that were perpetrated at the time. Do you believe that the Church now has an opportunity and responsibility to distance herself from contemporary injustice and wrong-doing by listening to, and entering into dialogue with, the Amazonian peoples?*
- *What for you was the most important point of the response of Pope Francis to the document on the Amazon? Do any of Sheila Curran's conclusions strike a particular chord with you?*

Endnotes

1. Pope Francis, *Querida Amazonia*, Vatican: Libreria Editrice Vaticana, 2020. Available at http://www.vatican.va/content/francesco/en/apost_exhortations/documents/papa-francesco_esortazione-ap_20200202_querida-amazonia.html; accessed 22 June 2022.

2. Synod of Bishops for the Pan-Amazon Region, *The Amazon: New Paths for the Church and for an Integral Ecology – Final Document*, Vatican: Libreria Editrice Vaticana, 2019. Available at http://secretariat.synod.va/content/sinodoamazonico/en/documents/final-document-of-the-amazon-synod.html; accessed 22 June 2022.

3. The preparatory document for the synod for the Amazon states, 'We begin with a specific geographical area in order to build a bridge to the other important biomes of our world: the Congo basin, the Mesoamerican Biological Corridor, the tropical forests of the Asia Pacific region, and the Guarani Aquifer, among others.' *Amazonia: New Paths for the Church and for an Integral Ecology: Preparatory Document of the Synod of Bishops for the Special Assembly for the Pan-Amazon Region*, Vatican: Libreria Editrice Vaticana, 2018, Preamble.

4. 'Pope Francis announces retrieval of indigenous statues', *Vatican News*, 25 October 2019. Available at https://www.vaticannews.va/en/pope/news/2019-10/pope-francis-comments-on-statues-stolen-from-church.html; accessed 22 June 2022.

5. Forty per cent of those killed worked on land, indigenous peoples and environmental rights. See Front Line Defenders, *Global Analysis 2019*, Dublin: Front Line, 2020. Available at https://www.frontlinedefenders.org/sites/default/files/global_analysis_2019_web.pdf; accessed 22 June 2022.

6. A system of corporate liability for human rights abuses is currently being negotiated in the UN. A revised draft of the legally binding instrument on business and human rights is available at https://www.ohchr.org/Documents/HRBodies/HRCouncil/WGTransCorp/OEIGWG_RevisedDraft_LBI.pdf; accessed 22 June 2022. The EU and Ireland have failed to support the treaty process so far.

7. See, for example, his address to seminarians on 24 November 2018 (as reported by Junno Arocho Esteves, 'Clericalism is Ugly Perversion, Pope Tells Seminarians', *Crux*, 26 November 2018. Available at https://cruxnow.com/vatican/2018/11/clericalism-is-ugly-perversion-pope-tells-seminarians; accessed 22 June 2022) and his letter to the people of God on 20 August 2018 (available at https://www.vatican.va/content/francesco/en/letters/2018/documents/papa-francesco_20180820_lettera-popolo-didio.html; accessed 22 June 2022).

THE SPIRITUAL CHALLENGES OF LATER LIFE

Una Agnew

Are the elderly really precious?
From the first mention of the Covid-19 pandemic in February 2020, it became clear that the ageing sector of the world's population was most at risk. The virus was particularly vicious towards those with less sturdy immune systems, respiratory fragility, slowing heart rates and dementia. Day after day, world statistics revealed that many in older age groups were losing the battle against the virus. All over seventy years of age were asked to stay at home, quarantined from visitors, and to venture out of doors only briefly for exercise and fresh air. In this way, the virus could be isolated and hopefully eradicated. 'The older age-group is precious, we must keep them safe. We want them to remain "cocooned" at home, where they will be safe and stop the spread of the virus.' Protection of the elderly became the daily watchword of medical and political teams alike, who, in daily progress reports issued words of encouragement during this universal lockdown period of the fateful spring and summer of 2020.

The attitude taken could so easily have been different: let the fittest survive and let all weaklings, already a burden on society, die! The Covid-19 pandemic has posed the deeper question for all of us concerning the value of older people. Are we older citizens 'precious' as stated, and are we a genuine asset to society? When I look out my window in suburban Dublin today, I see my eighty-year-old neighbour struggle to make his way to the shop for his daily newspaper. I wonder if he considers himself an asset to society. Who has time to stop and talk to him or does he just want to attend to his needs and disappear back into the solitude and/or loneliness of his retired life? How do we view the elderly in society and how do we ourselves deal with the reality of being numbered among the 'cocooned'?

Attitudes to ageing
There is a Japanese proverb that says: 'Receive age as a guest before you must surrender to age as a thief.' Yet, the attitude of welcoming one's elderly state and entertaining it as our guest runs counter to the prevailing Western culture, where age is feared as a burden to be avoided for as long as possible. Even the well-intended paternalism of 'Aren't you great!' is of little consolation, as if staying alive longer were a personal accomplishment! As a result of negative attitudes toward ageing, there is often a feverish compulsion to stay active for as long as possible, to work at physical fitness and mental alertness in the hope of keeping ageing at bay. But alas, physical decline, diminished status and social marginalisation are still the culturally accepted features typical of old age. As a result, those who are moving into the elderly age bracket tend to lose the expectation of looking forward to the joy and beauty inherent in growing old.[1]

Shakespeare has compounded the problem by his well-known, somewhat scathing portraits of the seven ages of man, played out on the stage of life, from the infant 'mewling and puking in the nurse's arms', to 'the lean and slippered pantaloon' of old age, that eventually degenerates into a mere phantom, lacking dignity, poise or vitality 'sans teeth, sans eyes, sans taste, sans everything'.[2] When Shakespeare wrote this, he himself was a young man, a talented outsider, bemused by stages of life of which he had little experience. His sonnet, 'Like as the Waves' (Sonnet 60) – despite its technical beauty – is equally sobering in its reminder that ageing steals the 'flourish set on youth | and delves the parallels in beauty's brow'. A sense of despondency induced by ageing touches everyone, since society at large is in love with youth culture. Yet, when asked themselves, older people are often quick to declare the present as the best time of their lives.[3] This does not mean that ageing is devoid of challenge. The ageing Hollywood film-star Bette Davis has proverbially declared: 'Old age is not for sissies!'

How to finally grow up
A popular saying maintains that 'growing *old* is mandatory; growing *up* is optional'! Carl Jung has laid the foundation for a definite programme of late-life psychology that proves there is still 'work' to be done as we age. Old age, he holds, cannot be just an appendage to an earlier active life; it has its own meaning in terms of growing into wholeness and finding one's soul-purpose in life. It is our final opportunity to reach individuation and the wholeness for which we were born. If we were to continue living in the same manner as we lived the first half of life, the energies of soul awaiting our exploration, would degenerate into the Yeatsian effigy of scarecrow or 'aged man', caricatured as nothing but 'a paltry thing | A tattered coat upon a stick'.[4]

The development of interiority with its greater concentration on *soul*, is the prerogative of later life. Soul must awaken and 'clap its hands and sing and louder sing' as a necessary antidote to ageing. In 'East Coker', T.S. Eliot also agrees that inner exploration is the task proper to later life when 'the world becomes stranger' and we grow into 'another intensity | for a further union, a deeper communion'.[5] Eliot is referring to growth in contemplation and union with God. Neglect of the opportunity to enter the realm of the Holy, at this time, can plunge a person into 'the void of nothingness'. Despair, then, can become the lot of many, who lose a sense of meaning, become depressed and fall into cynicism or nothingness.

More encouraging by far is the wisdom of psalm 92 which, in direct counter-cultural mode, asserts the possibility of a new springtime of life available to elders who rely on their rootedness in God to bring forth fruitfulness into their ageing years. 'They are planted in the house of the Lord; they flourish in the courts of our God. In old age they still produce fruit; they are always green and full of sap' (Ps 92:13-14). This potential for new life appropriate to old age is worth exploring further.

The Nautilus, an ancient sea-creature, a symbol of life's unfolding stages

The nautilus is one of the oldest living sea-creatures. It begins its life as a tiny creature visible at the centre of its spiral-shaped shell and grows through a series of ever-enlarging chambers. When it has outgrown a space, it leaves its current home and grows into a new space. Following its instinct, it fashions a new chamber, enlarging the shell as it goes and lining the new chamber with a substance secreted from within, to aid transition into the next stage of life. The nautilus' spiral is symbolic of life's unfolding mysteries. As we reflect on how our lives unfold, we notice more and more the mystery of God at work in our lives. We contemplate the many chambers of our lives we have inhabited, outgrown and moved on from as we have evolved toward new stages of life. The image of the spiral invites us to revisit any stage of our lives, pause, meditate, and receive again the knowledge, wisdom, and grace of that stage. Psalm 139 states: 'O Lord, you have searched me and known me. ... For it was you who formed my inward parts; you knit me together in my mother's womb' (Ps 139:1, 13). Revisiting the chambers of our lives is an opportunity to seek forgiveness, from ourselves and from others, 'for what I have done and what I have failed to do'.

Erikson's final stages of development require courage
In his classic work, *Childhood and Society*, Erik Erikson points to a sequence of eight stages of growth that, through specific psychological struggles, ultimately steer the person towards fullness of life from birth to death.[6] The first half of life's tasks have as their goal the building of a healthy ego with adequate social skills and the prospect of becoming a productive member of society. Within this schema, young adulthood has as its goal the development of a mature identity and an adult capacity for intimacy and love. The spiritual writer Richard Rohr holds that the first half of life simply builds the 'container' for our lives, while the task of the second half of life is 'to find the contents the container was meant to hold'.[7] How do we discover the life we were intended to live?

Two special developmental tasks that dignify later life
On a human level, Erikson dignifies later life with the demands of two significant tasks that challenge us to make our later years fulfilling and productive: generativity and wisdom.[8] The development of generativity as we approach our sixties and beyond initiates the process whereby we grow into a deeper capacity for the care of others and care for society at large.

Becoming generative rather than succumbing to stagnation can be the hallmark of a life desirous to pass on to the next generation the fruits of one's life in terms of learning, culture, faith, creativity and nurturance. Rather than stagnate in some state of well-earned comfort, we become aware of an impetus toward unconditional sharing of the fruits of one's life.

Mentoring others can be part of one's retired life. Encouragement is at the heart of mentoring. Edmund Rice spent his later years of retirement visiting classrooms in the Mount Sion school, where he liked nothing better than to hear the children answer questions and watch them grow into competent citizens. Far from adopting the role of supervisor or seeking the limelight as eminent founder of the Christian Brothers, he became an encouraging presence among teachers and students, revered simply for the sanctity of his presence. Mentoring promotes the well-being of others and rejoices in successes not our own.

The acquisition of wisdom

The acquisition of wisdom in later life belongs to the final phase of Erikson's stages of development. The older person, now in the seventy-plus age bracket, may begin to face the oncoming of physical diminishment, social isolation and feelings of uselessness. Doubts concerning the meaning of life begin to trigger despair or what James Loder refers to as descent into the void, a place of nothingness and loss of direction. Many succumb to this place of emptiness unless they recover their bearings or are guided in a counter direction towards the holy. Here they can often find comfort in the awareness of an ultimate horizon in their lives.[9]

Wisdom is best realisable when integrity confronts despair in the face of diminishment. An expanded consciousness is necessary to acquire wisdom. The assumed wisdom of old age is hard-earned and requires a process not normally associated with older people, a new level of growing up! Integrity will demand an honest facing-up to the truth about our lives, even their shadowy unredeemed recesses. Jungian scholar James Hollis has done excellent work in assisting people at this stage to come to terms with their shadow dimension as a preparation for fuller self-appropriation and growth in maturity.[10] Richard Rohr is also convinced that chronic negativity – seeing others as the cause of our unhappiness, wilful insistence on going our own way, begrudging the success of others and resentment at losses – all point to a neglect of personal shadow work. He himself prays for one humiliation a day to keep him honest in his life as minister of God. An expanded consciousness is necessary to plumb the unexplored regions of our souls. To navigate safely the potential region of despair in old age, and find one's pathway to serenity, one enters with St John of the Cross into its 'luminous darkness', wherein lies the peace of God.[11]

Coming to terms with the shadow dimension allows us to engage more freely in the harvesting of our lives. Erikson's wife Joan, who outlived her husband, was able, aged ninety, to add to her husband's theory, saying that the full flowering of human maturity comes from having confronted death and accepted the truth that wisdom is derived 'from life experience, well digested'. She is pointing towards a harvesting of life which depends on a new set of skills similarly proposed by Rabbi Schachter-Shalomi, whose book *From Age-ing to Sage-ing* describes how he himself learned that 'becoming older' can evolve into 'becoming elder'![12] Joan Erikson's insight into growing old has uncovered, perhaps, a *ninth* stage in human development, the stage of 'digesting life experience', distilling its lasting goodness.

The inner lining of our lives is what makes us precious
Erikson's approach to the developmental stages of life does not have an explicit theological perspective, whereas James Loder and Richard Rohr do. Writers in the area of Christian spirituality acknowledge that each stage of life is an invitation to graced living, to fashion one's life more closely in sync with the blueprint of God, the *imago Dei*, imprinted on our souls. As we age, we notice the slow work of God's divine forming mystery secretly at work at each stage of our lives, just as in each chamber of its growing life, the nautilus instinctively lines 'the walls' of its home with a delicate mother-of-pearl substance to enhance its living conditions. Each of us might pause to consider what constitutes the secret lining of our lives, particularly as we move into our wisdom years? What means do we use to grace our lives with inner resilience and meaning as we work at the task of life completion?

A rite of passage for elders
Experts today talk about eldering as the optimal process for mining the riches of old age to offset feelings and fears of diminishment and loneliness that many older people experience. Is there a rite of passage designed to help people make the necessary transition from older to elder? What would such a rite of passage look like? As he grew older, Rabbi Schachter-Shalomi realised the problem that confronted him and others who were beginning to deal with the realities of an extended lifespan. We are now living longer, and with this extended lifespan we need an extended consciousness. The process of growth into the state of becoming an elder is studied by Schachter-Shalomi and his colleague Robert Miller.[13]

Eldering is a challenging but hope-filled process necessary to render ageing not only bearable but meaningful and even enjoyable. On reaching retirement, each of us needs to take time off to embark on a process of initiation into old age that helps to liberate our spirit and plumb the depth of a wisdom that only now has matured and is ready to be explored. We need new skills to engage seriously with the art of life completion: confronting our death, harvesting the fruits of our lives, facing up to our shadow, letting go of hurts, practising forgiveness and giving thanks for life's blessings. This process also helps us envision a better future for humankind and a better stewardship of our planet earth.

We can point to the example of elders in Irish society that show us the way to a serene and productive old age. Edmund Rice was one who effectively modelled gratitude for his life's work as well as forgiveness for the hurts he endured throughout his enterprising life. His calm reliance on divine providence and trust in God were his gifts to those around him. There are also those living whom we could regard as elders, such as Mary Robinson, who is officially an elder of UN. There are others: President Michael D. Higgins, Sr Stan and Rev. Ruth Patterson, to mention but a few. Each of them wears the mantle of elder and speaks, as Mary Robinson does, with compassion for the poor, the marginalised and the dispossessed and addresses the needs of society and those of our planet earth. A cursory examination of their lives shows they have digested their life experiences and distilled for themselves and others a mentoring wisdom that benefits all. As a renowned elder, now in his mid-eighties, Charles Handy has placed the learnings of his life in the form of twenty-one letters written to his grandchildren. His recent publication sums up what he now sees as contemporary challenges for entrepreneurs, dreamers and citizens of the future.[14] Mistakes and successes honestly digested are sources of wisdom for others.

Conclusion: The real challenges of ageing

At the beginning of this paper I asked the question, 'Are old people really precious?' I have turned the question back towards all of us over seventy, asked to 'cocoon' during the pandemic. Health specialists and government officials were equally solicitous for our well-being. Meanwhile, many of us in this category stubbornly resisted being receptors of care and, on occasion, reacted to being non-productive at a time of national emergency as if we could revert to a lifestyle suited to an earlier stage of life. What have we learned? Do we still persist with the question 'What is the value of a life past retirement?'

Longevity or extended age span, we have discovered, requires an expanded consciousness if we are to live our final years fruitfully. While keeping fit and taking normal care of health and diet is essential, dealing with our psychology and spirituality is even more important. The transformation from older into elder commits us to a serious harvesting of our lives, not in terms of possessions, but in terms of *generative* living, graced with integrity, wisdom and gratitude. We need a new skillset to help us expand our consciousness and make us capable of dealing with our past, practicing forgiveness and healing our own lives before addressing the healing of our planet earth. Unnecessary baggage can weigh down the ageing self, whereas acceptance of brokenness and honest recognition of our shadow self leads to wisdom and an understanding of others. It is the depth of our spirituality that will guide us into the newness of spirit promised by psalm 91. Exploring the contemplative power awaiting us in areas of the brain that only now are becoming accessible brings freshness to our lives. Rather than pine for youth, or wallow in despair, we enter with St John of the Cross into that 'luminous darkness' where we find a new expanded consciousness and, in the words of Cardinal Newman, 'a safe lodging, and a holy rest':

> May He support us all the day long,
> till the shades lengthen,
> and the evening comes,
> and the busy world is hushed,
> and the fever of life is over,
> and our work is done!
> Then in His mercy
> may He give us a safe lodging,
> and a holy rest,
> and peace at the last![15]

Reflection
- *Did it really take the Covid-19 pandemic for us to consider the place of the elderly in our societies?*
- *Does our culture define old age in terms of physical frailty, limitations and social marginalisation? Do we – like Edmund Rice – see beyond vulnerability and recognise the fundamental dignity and precious giftedness of each person?*
- *What do you make of the distinction between growing old and growing up, and do you see old age as a time for personal growth and the development of a deeper relationship with the Divine?*
- *Having read this chapter, do you clearly see the old as precious and as possessing integrity and wisdom?*
- *Do you know of anyone who was mentored by an older person or who benefited by mentoring from an older person?*

Endnotes

1. On this, see Vern L. Bengtson and Joseph A. Kuypers, 'Generational Difference and the Development Stake', *The International Journal of Aging and Human Development*, Vol. 2, No. 4, 1971, pp 249–60. https://doi.org/10.2190/AG.2.4.b.
2. William Shakespeare, *As You Like It*, Act 2, Scene 7.
3. Cf. Henry S. Maas and Joseph A. Kuypers, 'From Thirty to Seventy', San Francisco: Jossey-Bass, 1974.
4. W.B. Yeats, 'On Sailing to Byzantium', *The Tower*, London: Macmillan, 1928.
5. T.S. Eliot, 'East Coker', *Four Quartets*, London: Faber and Faber, 1943. Used with permission.
6. Erik H. Erikson, *Childhood and Society*, New York: W.W. Norton, 1963.
7. Richard Rohr, 'On the Two Halves of Life', *Patheos*, 2 February 2015. Available at www.patheos.com/blogs/emergentvillage/2015/02/the-two-halves-of-life; accessed 28 July 2022.
8. Erik H. Erikson, Joan M. Erikson and Helen Q. Kivnick, *Vital Involvement in Old Age,* New York: W.W. Norton, 1986.
9. On this, see James E. Loder, *The Logic of the Spirit: Human Development in Theological Perspective*, San Francisco: Jossey-Bass Publishers, 1998.
10. See James Hollis, *Finding Meaning in the Second Half of Life: How to Finally Really Grow Up*, New York: Gotham Books, 2005. See also Reboot Podcast, 'Episode #51 – The Love that Heals: Welcoming in our Shadow – with James Hollis', 21 November 2016. Available at https://www.reboot.io/episode/51-the-love-that-heals-shadow-james-hollis/; accessed 5 July 2022.
11. Saint John of the Cross, quoted in Richard Rohr, 'A Bright Sadness', in *Falling Upward: A Spirituality for the Two Halves of Life*, San Francisco: Jossey-Bass, 2011, pp. 117–25.
12. Zalman Schachter-Shalomi and Ronald S. Miller, *From Age-ing to Sage-ing: A Revolutionary Approach to Growing Older,* New York: Grand Central Publishing, 2014.
13. Ibid., pp. 79–184.
14. Charles Handy, *21 Letters on Life and its Challenges*, London: Penguin Random House, 2019.
15. John Henry Newman, 'Sermon XX: Wisdom and Innocence', in *Sermons Bearing on Subjects of the Day*, London: Rivingtons, 1869, p. 307.

LOVE THROUGH LITTLE WINDOWS: REFLECTIONS ON THE PARADOX AND POWER OF VULNERABILITY

Maria Garvey

> For God's foolishness is wiser than human wisdom, and God's weakness is stronger than human strength.
> (1 Corinthians 1:25)

Covid-19: Tearing a hole in the familiar fabric of our lives and glimpsing what is real

The concept of 'fellowships of fragile humanity' has fascinated me for as long as I can remember. From recovery and support groups to L'Arche communities committed to revealing the gifts of people with disabilities, they all have a quality of openhearted humanity that I love. I've spent more than half of my life in L'Arche and though I no longer have an organisational role, I'm still very much connected to our community in Belfast. Beyond that, my work these days focuses on what it takes to be fully human together and embrace our vulnerability as a source of life, unity and healing in the world. I write this in the middle of the Covid-19 lockdown. Rarely in our lifetime have we experienced the pain and the power of our shared vulnerability as acutely as during this pandemic. In a matter of days, our normal worldview was turned on its head and the global spread of a novel coronavirus brought us to a standstill. Tearing a hole in the familiar fabric of our lives, it allowed us to glimpse what is most real. We learned that few things actually matter and we learned just how much those few things do matter – a hug, a bird singing, a seed sprouting, sunshine on our skin, the touch of a loved one, a word from a friend, a gift of banana bread, a toilet roll! Our relationship with space and time shifted, making room for one of life's essential questions: Who am I when I am not what I do? If the pandemic has taught us anything, it's that the dance between our strength and our vulnerability is what makes us truly human. We are all invited into that dance, and when we recognise our need for one another and dare to step out together, we become a fellowship of vulnerable, open-hearted humanity where everyone belongs.

What better time than now to experience and explore what it is to be vulnerable together and allow ourselves to be led by people who, by virtue of illness and disability, can show us the way into the deeper dimensions of what it means to be fully human – fragile and free, weak and strong, alone and together all at the same time. These unlikely leaders have been my companions and teachers for over forty years and have graciously allowed me to accompany them through the most vulnerable and sacred moments of their lives. For that, I am deeply grateful. Shortly I'll see some of their faces on one of our regular 'Zoom Café' gatherings. Their unbridled excitement through tiny online windows is a tonic, a powerful antidote to the isolation of lockdown and a contagion of love that heals not hurts, blesses not bruises and can touch, move and connect people across vast distances.

Not for the first time, I find myself wondering: how can it be that people, who seem to have so little to offer the world, have so much to heal it?

God makes no mistakes
Caroline had a rare condition. Uremic poisoning caused her to have what we referred to as 'itchy-brain syndrome'. In an effort to relieve that itch she relentlessly thumped her temples until they bruised. By the age of four her arms were secured to her wheelchair, she wore a helmet to protect her head from the trauma of constant hitting and a gum-shield to protect her bottom lip from being bitten. No matter what anyone did Caroline's 'itchy brain' persisted and all she could do was cry. From morning to night those piercing cries were all she had to offer the world.

Dennis O'Toole was a member of the Legion of Mary, a Catholic lay apostolic movement, and he visited the clinic regularly. On one such visit he knelt down in front of Caroline's wheelchair, gently lifted her curly head and sang the chorus of a song he had composed especially for her:

> The smallest flower,
> The tallest tree,
> They have a job to do for Thee,
> To show the world Your majesty,
> Oh Lord, have you a job for me?

'God makes no mistakes, Caroline,' he whispered, 'and God knows that you are doing your job just perfectly'. Caroline died not long after that day. It was a happy release from her seven years of anguish. A few years later Dennis died from cancer, alone in his own home. 'Two insignificant lives,' one might say, 'what real difference did they make?'

Well, here's the thing: forty years after her death, from Belfast to Bangalore, Madras to Mexico, people all over the world are still singing Caroline's song. It seems that whenever and wherever people hear the story of Caroline and Dennis, they're moved to stand up and sing. Perhaps they remind us that the difference we make is not in the work that we do, but in the love that we generate. Such vulnerable love touches us. It disarms our hearts and challenges all that de-humanises our world. Such naked love lives on long beyond our lifetimes.

All of your heart

> If you seek me with all of your heart, I will let you find me. (Jer 29:13-14)

I've witnessed the power of vulnerability to heal, connect and transform people's lives in many different circumstances and conditions but, yet, not for one moment do I want to spiritualise or romanticise it. The word 'vulnerable', according to the Merriam-Webster dictionary, is ultimately derived from the Latin *vulnerare*, meaning 'to wound', and let's face it, who but the bravest or most foolish among us would willingly open themselves to being wounded? Coming face to face with our vulnerability is rarely a choice; it's often very scary, and for the most part we'll do anything to avoid it.

Many of us learned from an early age how to 'behave ourselves' so as not to risk losing the love of a parent or caregiver. Our survival depended on denying the parts of ourselves that didn't make people happy. Gradually over time we learned how to keep our fears and our fragilities hidden and, as the old saying goes, we grew accustomed to keeping the best side out. By the time we get to adulthood, we already have a lifetime of defending and pretending behind us and carry a deep-seated fear that someday, somehow, someone will see through us and discover that we are imposters. The effort to 'look good' all the time, while it might gain us admiration, can cost us intimacy and love. Paradoxically, what we most want to hide about ourselves may well be the doorway through which we find joy, freedom and wholeness.

That said, perhaps our greatest fear is not that we will be wounded or 'exposed as imposters'; perhaps deeper down again, where we rarely dare to go, we are all afraid that we're not enough and fundamentally unlovable. Perhaps that's the lie that we've mistaken for the truth and we spend a lifetime protecting ourselves from the unbearable pain of it. It seems to me that it's our longing to love and to be loved that makes us most vulnerable. I was speaking to a friend recently, the father of a little girl with significant disabilities – 'the most amazing thing about Lucy' he said 'is that she never doubts that she's loved. She comes with arms outstretched and expects to be met by love wherever she goes'. What a blessing.

'Remain here, and stay awake with me' (Mt 26:38)
Learning to trust in love took a lot longer for Joe. By the time he and I first encountered one another, he had already spent over thirty years in different institutional care settings, from the mother and baby home where he was born to the lock-up ward of the large psychiatric hospital where he now lived. All his life he had looked through the windows of ordinary houses on ordinary streets and seen glimpses of the kind of family he wanted for himself. He longed to live in 'a proper house, with roast chicken on the bone and a fire that would burn if you put your hand in it'! From his shirt pocket he drew out a disintegrating picture of Jesus that apparently he'd been given by the priest who gave him his first Holy Communion. 'Jesus is here,' he told me, 'he always looks after me.' That priest had visited him regularly in the children's home, but in the end he – like everyone else in Joe's life – finally left him too.

After a lifetime of rejection and abandonment, coming to live in L'Arche was an act of pure bravery for Joe and a sign of his unquenchable hope. In the beginning, everything went well. We delighted in him and he delighted in home life. However, as the months passed and relationships deepened, Joe's anguish increased and soon his behaviour was so challenging that it didn't seem possible for us to continue living with him. The stress of having to be good all the time so that we wouldn't give up on him became so overwhelming for Joe it made him ill and it was clear that he needed more help than we could give him. As we walked through the hospital double doors, he clung for dear life to my sleeve begging over and over 'Please, please Mahwee, don't send me away. I'll be good'. Given how often his trust had been betrayed, it's little wonder he didn't trust the assurances that we would come back for him. He loosened his grip and walked towards the ward like a lamb to the slaughter. During the next three weeks, we busied ourselves painting his bedroom yellow (his favourite colour) and visited him every day. On the day he finally came back, he looked around his newly painted bedroom, then looked at all of us: 'Yellow!' he proclaimed, joyfully. 'I'm home and you're still here.'

Amazingly, the damage that life had done to Joe's heart was not beyond repair. Maybe his resilience came from his lifelong trust in a Jesus who would never give up on him. I don't know, but what I can say for sure is that from that day to this one, Joe has not looked back. These days, he's happy to be himself with all of the hope and the heartache mixed up together inside of him. Today, all over the world, there are people who love him just as he is and he continues to flourish and rejoice in their friendship. 'No matter how bad I get, will you still stay?' was the unspoken cry of Joe's heart. I sometimes think that that's the deepest cry in all of us.

Love Through Little Windows

To be human is to be vulnerable

To be human is to be vulnerable, and perhaps it's simply a matter of being willing to take the risk of being fully ourselves and loving what we love without holding back. Geoffrey didn't know the meaning of holding back. He loved life, every single morsel of it. For him, each moment was a celebration, and anyone lucky enough to be in his company couldn't help but celebrate too. He came to live with us in L'Arche when he was thirty years old and died when he was thirty-three. I love to think of those three years as his public ministry. His funeral was an extraordinary celebration of what appeared to be a very ordinary life. People came from far and wide and from all walks of life. The postman, the bin men, the pharmacist, Church leaders, neighbours, local shopkeepers, people of every colour, hue and political persuasion all turned up to bid their final farewell. Before long the galleries and even the sanctuary were filled and still people kept coming until they spilled out into the driveway. It was the biggest funeral the church had ever seen.

'How come you're here today?' I whispered to a bishop as I ushered him into the Church. 'How could I not be,' he replied, 'every time I met Geoffrey he welcomed me like I was melted chocolate.' How little he knew just how true that was! You see Geoffrey adored chocolate but sadly he was nearly always on a diet! However, he quickly discovered that if he invited people into our kitchen for a wee cup of tea, they were sure to be offered chocolate biscuits, and as he entertained them with his four-stringed guitar and his fascination with car keys and Mini Coopers, he happily munched his way through plateful after plateful of biscuits!

Nobody was immune to his invitation, and those who came in as strangers went out as friends. Geoffrey never in his life set out to be good. For him being good was simply a given. He never planned to make a difference. No, Geoffrey was

191

just himself: delightful, excitable, joyful, insatiable and, from time to time, a wee bit greedy! Whenever I think about him now, I smile, remembering how many hearts he melted and healed by simply loving what he loved. Life surely doesn't get much sweeter than that!

In the end 'there is need of only one thing' (Lk 10:42)
Like Martha in the Christian gospels, some of us are distracted by our need to be in control and we spend far too many precious moments worrying and fretting about things that may never happen. In all of that commotion, it's easy to lose sight of what really matters, and at the end of our lives, we may discover that we've passed through this life without ever having really lived at all. If we have ears to hear Caroline, Joe, Lucy, Geoffrey and all those others who encounter the world with undefended hearts, we might hear them whisper, 'Just be yourself in every moment and trust that that's enough':

> God chose what is foolish in the world to shame the wise; God chose what is weak in the world to shame the strong; God chose what is low and despised in the world, things that are not, to reduce to nothing things that are. (1 Cor 1:27-9)

From his burning bush experience the apostle Paul knew this, and in a similar way I imagine that Blessed Edmund Rice did too. The untimely death of his wife and the eternal innocence of his daughter would have broken open his heart and given him eyes to see and be moved by the raw humanity he witnessed in the streets outside his window.

As I write this reflection, I'm grateful for the opportunity to be with my own humanity with tenderness now and it seems to me that vulnerability may simply be the courage to show up for life just as it is and just as I am, one moment at a time. Embracing my vulnerability gives me a clearer and more compassionate lens through which to view the world around me. It opens my eyes to see beyond what is visible and stretches my heart so that I too can be fully seen. To be vulnerable is to live with my heart laid open, holding nothing in, keeping nothing out. It is a resounding 'amen' to life, a radical acceptance of all that is, all that has been and all that will ever be. When all is said and done, it seems to me that love is the one thing that matters and that the purpose of our lives is to learn how to love. Remembering the generous teachers who invited me into their hearts, loved me in all the ways that I needed to be loved and allowed me to love them back, it occurs to me now that vulnerability may simply be another name for love.

Reflection
- *In our modern world, with its cult of perfection, health and beauty, those who are elderly, frail, vulnerable and those who have disabilities or are otherwise deemed to be 'different' are often considered as 'other than us' and may even be viewed with fear and suspicion. Though no longer hidden away, they may still be invisible to eyes that cannot see behind the labels that diminish and dehumanise us all. Yet in the L'Arche communities Maria Garvey encountered the authentic vulnerability, dignity and healing humanity of people who welcomed her into their hearts and loved her unconditionally.*
- *In what ways might I be 'blind' to the dignity and humanity of those in the margins by simply seeing them as an unwelcome reminder of my own vulnerability or a reason to be grateful for my own blessings?*
- *What helps me to drop my barriers and open my heart to those who are different from me so that I recognise our shared humanity in a way that touches, connects and blesses us?*

- *Who are the people in my life with whom I feel free to be fully myself and truly embrace my own vulnerability as a gift rather than a weakness?*

LIFTING THE VEIL AND RESTORING COMPASSION TO OUR EYES

Aidan Donaldson

> If I encounter a person sleeping outdoors on a cold night, I can view him or her as an annoyance, an idler, an obstacle in my path, a troubling sight, a problem for politicians to sort out, or even a piece of refuse cluttering a public space. Or I can respond with faith and charity and see in this person a human being with a dignity identical to my own, a creature infinitely loved by the Father, an image of God, a brother or sister redeemed by Jesus Christ.[1]

How we see others is a window that reveals much about who we are as individuals, as a society and as people. It pierces our deepest essence and holds a mirror to our relationship with self, others and God. It shines a light into and onto our inner selves and illuminates our very souls. It tells us who we are and what we are. It is both a remarkable and terrifying thing. The challenge of the gospel is always directed primarily at each of us and how we act towards those we encounter – especially those in the margins. This is how we are to be judged as Jesus warns in the parable of the final judgement in Matthew's Gospel when he states that 'just as you did it to one of the least of these who are members of my family, you did it to me' (Mt 25:40). And so we are told, in no uncertain terms, that we will be judged – both as individuals and as societies – on our treatment of anyone who is hungry, thirsty, a foreigner, naked, sick or imprisoned. This is not an optional extra or choice; rather it is an imperative, an inescapable duty of being a Christian. It is what Pope Francis might call the hallmark of Christian discipleship – 'the beating heart of the Gospel'. Pope Francis, quoting St John Paul II says:

> The text of Matthew 25:35-6 is 'not a simple invitation to charity: it is a page of Christology which sheds a ray of light on the mystery of Christ'. In this call to recognise him in the poor and the suffering ... given these uncompromising demands of Jesus, it is my duty to ask Christians to acknowledge and accept them in a spirit of genuine openness, *sine glossa*. ... Our Lord made it very clear that holiness cannot be understood or lived apart from these demands, for mercy is 'the beating heart of the Gospel'.[2]

Sometimes we respond to the challenge of discipleship by regarding who Jesus commands us to embrace as our brothers and sisters as objects of our pity – in other words by acting as if it is *they* (the people in the margins) who are in need of *our* help. So, we come to think of ourselves as 'messiahs' or 'saviours' who can use our power to help those in need while the poor and marginalised are regarded as passive recipients of our charitable actions. Yet there is so much more to this than viewing the world thus. In fact, the challenge of the gospel as encapsulated in Matthew 25 involves a reversal and complete transformation in our thinking. Perhaps it is us – the apparently comfortable and 'respectable' people (and often deemed so in terms of religious practice and social status) – who need the 'outsiders' and 'rejected' for *our* salvation. The kingdom of God announced by Jesus implies and necessitates nothing less than a revolution in our thinking and acting and in our relationship between ourselves and those in the margins and, indeed, with God. It requires a move from 'charity' to 'compassion', of seeing others (and especially the poor) as our brothers and sisters, as God's reflections, as ourselves. Jesus showed this through his teachings, actions and example. We are told to 'be merciful, just as your Father is merciful' (Lk 6:36). Indeed, if we are to be true to the call to be a disciple, we must be prepared to refocus and transform our lives according to the needs of those in need. To do otherwise is to ignore God himself.

Pope Francis identifies the Beatitudes as the key teaching in which Jesus gives us in the clearest and most unambiguous terms what God demands of us. They are 'a Christian's identity card. … a portrait of the Master which we are called to reflect in our daily lives'.[3] The God we are called on to serve and imitate is the God of the forsaken, the God of universal hope and unconditional love who loves the poor, the afflicted and marginalised. It is in and through 'the least of these' that we encounter God.

So what did Edmund see when he looked through the window?

More than two hundred years ago, in the dark days following his wife's tragic death, Edmund Rice was gazing out of a window in Waterford and contemplating living out the rest of his life in a monastery in Europe. He was on the cusp of withdrawing from the world – a world full of heartbreak and pain – when his attention was drawn by his close friend, Mary Power, to presence of groups of impoverished young people who were wandering aimlessly around the docks of the town. They were indeed the 'wretched of the earth' who were despised, excluded and lost – even to themselves. Yet he did not see them simply as poor, unfortunate children who were in need of help and support – although they certainly were that. Edmund saw them as children of God, created in his image and likeness, and saw in them the very presence of Christ. He looked at them through eyes of compassion and saw in them a dignity befitting a child of God, and he sought for that dignity to be realised and affirmed in their daily lives.

We often confuse or conflate the Christian sense of compassion with a feeling of sorrow or sadness for the suffering of others. And while it does include this, it goes far beyond it. Compassion is not about seeing people in need, feeling sorry for them and then acting out of a sense of duty or sentiment. It is about seeing them as our brothers and sisters and taking on their pain as our own pain in the same way a parent feels the pain of their child. It presupposes a new sense of love based on a unity with the other and a living out of this radical love as exemplified by Jesus' love for us and expressed by Paul in his First Letter to the Corinthians when he reminds us that we are all members of 'one body' and that 'if one member suffers, all suffer together with it' (1 Cor 12:12, 26). Compassion is a liberating action. It abolishes the distinction between 'us' and 'them', between the 'self' and the 'other'. Instead, I become you, you become me, and we become one. It is an emptying of the self and an embracing of the sense of *communitas*, of the oneness that Jesus established through the Eucharist, through which we become united with each other and with God. Pope Francis describes compassion as follows:

> Compassion allows you to see reality; compassion is like the lens of the heart: it allows us to take in

and understand the true dimensions. In the Gospels, Jesus is often moved by compassion. And compassion is also the language of God.[4]

Jesus and compassion
Time and time again, Jesus used 'the language of God' in his interactions with those in need. Throughout his mission in Galilee and last days in Jerusalem, Jesus actively sought out those whom society had ignored, excluded and condemned as unworthy of God's favour. Lepers; widows and orphans; those suffering from disability, mental torment and poverty; women; sinners, including prostitutes and tax collectors – these, the very people who society rejected as unworthy, were precisely those who Jesus told were the heirs to the kingdom of God. He saw them not just through eyes of pity and sorrow but of compassion and love. He saw them as children of God and in them, God's very presence. It was among them – and not the Temple or synagogues, or the 'respectable people' – that he centred his revolution of love. One particular episode in Luke's Gospel (7:36-55) is a clear illustration of this.

We are told that Jesus was invited to the house of Simon the Pharisee as an honoured guest at dinner. A most important occasion indeed, but one which was disrupted by the presence of a woman – and not just any woman but one 'who was a sinner'. We are told that she washed Jesus' feet with her tears, dried them with her hair and anointed them with a jar of extremely expensive perfume. Naturally, Simon was outraged (as, presumably, would have been all the other guests). After all, 'If this man were a prophet, he would know who and what kind of woman this is who is touching him – that she is a sinner.' Yet far from objecting to the woman's actions, Jesus praises her for her 'great love' that proves that her many sins have been forgiven, and, making Simon and the rest of the guests even more uncomfortable and outraged, tells the woman, 'Your faith has saved you; go in peace.'

Perhaps one might reflect on the idea that Simon – the respectable Pharisee – has much in common with a ritualised, judgemental, unthinking and clericalised version of Church, whereas the encounter between Jesus and the woman reveals and anticipates a missionary Church that is dynamic, non-judging, critical and liberating – a Church that truly reflects a God of compassion and love.

If Edmund looked out the window today, what would he see?

If Edmund Rice looked out the window today, he would see a much-changed Ireland. A country once ravaged by hunger and whose people had been forced into a state of abject poverty, distress and hopelessness is now one of the wealthiest countries in the world.[5] And this great change owes much to Edmund and those who, inspired by his example, joined him in the Christian Brothers and Presentation Brothers. It is well demonstrated that education is the key to social transformation and improvement. Edmund, and all those who followed his example, have played a huge role in Ireland and numerous other countries in this regard.

And yet Edmund might also be saddened and bewildered – even angry perhaps – at what he would see in modern Ireland today. A country now wealthy beyond the wildest dreams of those only a generation or two ago still tolerates great poverty, suffering and hopelessness among many in our society. In every city, town and village in Ireland there are people who experience real poverty. There are countless numbers of people who are homeless and hungry, people who are excluded, alienated and marginalised, including people in prison, ex-offenders, victims of alcohol and drug abuse, migrants, people with poor mental health and the unemployed. Like much of the rest of the apparently affluent world, it seems that, in modern Ireland, care for those in need is not high on the political agenda. The words of the Early Church Father St John Chrysostom might be lost on those in power in today's Ireland: 'Not to share one's wealth with the poor is to steal from them and to take away their livelihood. It is not our own goods which we hold, but theirs.'[6]

Modern Ireland: No longer a land of saints, scholars and missionaries

There was a time in the not too distant past when the words 'Irish' and 'Catholic' were often inseparable. Ireland had been almost defined by its religious practice and missionary outreach. Sunday Mass attendance was the norm, and almost every family seemed to have a relative who was a priest or religious either in Ireland or in the missions. In recent years, this has changed dramatically. The country long-described as *'Hibernia semper fides'* is now a new Ireland scarcely distinguishable from many other Western societies. Compassion, community, love of the other and a search for God have been replaced by a new set of pre-eminent values that are, in essence, non-religious (indeed, even anti-religious) including secularism, materialism, pursuit of wealth, consumerism and individualism. Pope Francis points out the contrast thus: 'The world tells us to seek success, power and money; God tells us to seek humility, service and love.'[7] As a society, we now experience (and often promote) a pernicious and all-pervading spiritual poverty in which relationship with our self, others and God is undermined and pushed to the margins. This paradigm shift has had enormous implications on how Western society views and treats its members and especially the vulnerable, ill, frail and elderly as witnessed in the recent Covid-19 pandemic and the seeming lack of attention given to the plight of the elderly in care homes.

This pandemic has lightened the darkness beneath our structures that has propelled disparities throughout societies and the world. One of the darkest evils that exists with banality is the absolute lack of empathy or solidarity with the other. Thus, our frail and elderly are viewed as weak, complaining and dispensable. In a similar fashion, many migrants and refugees fleeing poverty, famine and oppression – as well as brutal wars in countries such as Syria, Afghanistan and Ukraine – often find themselves ignored, uncared for or viewed with suspicion and sometimes hostility. Ireland, for so many years a centre of missionary outreach and compassion, is now new missionary territory itself. No longer a country of extraordinary practice and faith, it would seem that the hopelessness and despair that Edmund saw when he looked out the window in Waterford more than two hundred years ago has returned. Affluence has indeed come to Ireland – but at a considerable price.

Becoming missionary and seeing anew
Throughout his papacy Pope Francis has urged all who wish to follow Christ to embrace the call to become 'missionary disciples' and to create a missionary Church as envisaged and initiated by Jesus himself. We, all of us, through our baptism, are called to be missionaries, disciples who have encountered God's love and must dare to go into the world and announce the Good News.[8] Without this we are mere 'pastry-shop Christians … delectable but not real Christians'.[9] By this, Pope Francis suggests that many of us simply go *to* Church and not *from* Church. Do we go to Mass and keep God's law and the commands and rules of the Church without reflecting on

our own sacred vocation – one that is given to each single member of the Church on our baptism? Have we embraced a safe, 'privatised' or 'comfortable' form of Christianity that permits us to follow a path without sacrifice, without risk, without the cross?

It is precisely this that the great German theologian Dietrich Bonhoeffer cautioned against when he distinguished between 'cheap grace' – grace without discipleship, grace without the cross – and 'costly grace' – the grace of the gospel which calls us to 'take up the cross' and follow Christ.[10] 'Cheap grace', he adds, 'is the deadly enemy of our church ... sold on the market like cheapjacks' wares.' In a similar vein, Pope Francis urges us to 'embrace the cross' and renounce wealth and worldliness, which is crushing the very soul of all of us and the Church itself:

> Jesus himself told us: 'You cannot serve two masters: either you serve God or you serve mammon' (cf. Mt 6:24). In mammon itself there is this worldly spirit; money, vanity, pride, that path ... we cannot take it ... It is unthinkable that a Christian – a true Christian – be it a priest, a sister, a bishop, a cardinal or a Pope, would want to go down this path of worldliness ... Spiritual worldliness kills! It kills the soul! It kills the person! It kills the Church![11]

The pursuit of wealth and worldliness destroy our ability to know ourselves, to recognise others as brothers and sisters and to develop our relationship with God. Liberated from this, we are able to bear witness to the gospel and become the missionary Church that could then 'go', as Jesus commissioned, 'make disciples of all nations' (Mt 28:19).

Where will we encounter this missionary Church and what might it look like?

In the Sermon on the Mount, Jesus looked at his audience – the marginalised, the broken and the rejected – and announced that 'theirs is the kingdom of Heaven' (Mt 5:3). And so it was for Edmund when he looked through eyes of compassion and set about on his mission. It was among the poor, the abandoned and those without hope – what the French West Indian writer Frantz Fanon called 'the wretched of the earth'[12] – that he recognised God and placed his mission. Perhaps if we had the same courage as Edmund and removed the veil from our eyes to look with compassion at the world today, we would see each person as a brother and sister – the very living presence of Christ himself. Then we might dare to imagine new ways of living and being for one another, of announcing the Good News with joy as befitting missionary disciples, of seeking to create the kingdom in the here and now through compassion and love. In this way, we will make the Father's will 'be done on earth as it is in heaven'.

Reflection
- *When Edmund's attention was drawn to the plight of the poor children in front of him, he ceased to gaze. Instead he looked, he saw, he was moved, and he acted. How often do we gaze out of our own 'windows on the world' and do not see because we are too wrapped up in our own lives?*
- *Do we look but do not see because what we might see might disturb us – or do we see but do not act because it is somebody's else's problem?*
- *Every single day we encounter people in need. Do we stop and look deep into their eyes with compassion and recognise them as our brother or sister as Edmund did or do we continue to gaze into space and just ignore them?*

Endnotes

1 Pope Francis, *Gaudete et Exsultate*, 98.
2 Ibid., 96–7.
3 Ibid., 63.
4 Pope Francis, quoted in Linda Bordini, 'Pope at Mass: Compassion is the Language of God', *Vatican News*, 17 September 2019. Available at www.vaticannews.va/en/pope-francis/mass-casa-santa-marta/2019-09/pope-francis-homily-casa-santa-marta-compassion.html; accessed 8 July 2022.
5 Ireland is cited in numerous financial journals and reports as one of the richest countries in the world according to a range of generally universally accepted wealth criteria such as Gross Domestic Product (GDP). See, for example, Garrett Parker, 'The 20 Richest Countries in Europe', *Money Inc*, 2019. Available at https://moneyinc.com/richest-countries-in-europe-in-2019; accessed 8 July 2022.
6 Saint John Chrysostom, *De Lazaro Concio*, II, 6: PG 48, 992D; quoted in Pope Francis, *Evangelii Gaudium*, 57.
7 Pope Francis, quoted in Alicia von Stamwitz (ed.), *The Spirit of St Francis: Inspiring Words on Faith, Love and Creation*, New York: SPCK, 2015, p. 105.
8 See, for example, *Evangelii Gaudium*, 120.
9 Pope Francis, quoted in Robert P. Imbelli, 'Pastry Shop Christians', *Commonweal*, 4 October 2013. Available at www.commonwealmagazine.org/pastry-shop-christians; accessed 8 July 2022.
10 Dietrich Bonhoeffer, *The Cost of Discipleship*, New York: MacMillan, 1963, p. 26.
11 Pope Francis, Address at Meeting with the Poor Assisted by Caritas, 4 October 2013. Available at https://www.vatican.va/content/francesco/en/speeches/2013/october/documents/papa-francesco_20131004_poveri-assisi.html; accessed 8 July 2022.
12 Frantz Fanon, *The Wretched of the Earth*, Harmondsworth: Penguin, 1961.

LEARN TO LIVE TOGETHER AS BROTHERS AND SISTERS OR PERISH AS FOOLS

Martin Byrne

Edmund Rice looking out the window
Edmund looked out the window and saw and felt the shame of struggling humanity. There are essentially two contrasting ways of looking out the window on to the street: from the 'real' perspective of the powerful or from the piteous, 'ridiculous' stance of people living in acute poverty. What we see depends upon where we stand and upon the filters we keep on our glasses. My vision at times is restricted and hardened when coloured with my male, educated, entitled and Western lenses. Our middle-class gaze seals and shields us from discomfort. Edmund Rice's heart was broken open by the truth of hunger and poverty, and he pushed out against the normalised zone of acceptability. Edmund's gospel vision, which inspired the hearts of others, saw wild flowers springing-up in the harsh wastelands of Waterford's muddy back lanes. Driven by an entrepreneurial heart of concern, Edmund Rice put flesh and scaffolding on the gospel impulse to liberate and be brothers and sisters to those around us. Our global society today remains famished for a brothering and sistering community of justice.

Deadly inward gaze

Martin Luther King Jr cautioned us to learn to live together as brothers or perish together as fools. Today, when we rub the sleep from our eyes, befriend the leper within and see life through the lenses of the experiences of poor people, then we can proclaim liberty. The implications of looking out the window with the eyes of Edmund are costly. It requires of us to empty ourselves of our credentials and to identify in kinship and presence with people who struggle. Unfortunately, such action for justice is a peripheral activity in Church and society, and until such time that Christians show a commitment to indiscriminate welcome and to make that pledge to justice a priority, then the gospel vision of God remains silenced and the voices of the poor muzzled. With Christ crucified and impotent, we opt to stand, and sometimes it is our profound prophetic deportment to be the tears of the clown: to feel the pain, to moan, sigh, curse, cry and ask awkward questions. One such question for me is how best to be a brother or sister in today's hurting world?[1]

Pope Francis' appeal to look outwards towards a 'poor Church of the poor'

Pope Francis urged Catholic priests at the Chrism Mass on Holy Thursday in 2016 to devote themselves to helping the poor and suffering instead of worrying about careers as Church 'managers':

> It is not in soul-searching or constant introspection that we encounter the Lord. ... We need to go out, then, in order to experience our own anointing ... to the outskirts where there is suffering, bloodshed, blindness that longs for sight, and prisoners in thrall to many evil masters. ... Those who do not go out

of themselves, instead of being mediators, gradually become intermediaries, managers.[2]

What follows are five different yet related expressions of how I perceive the charism of Edmund Rice and the vision of Pope Francis to be enfleshed and lived at the edges of Irish society today.

1. Neighbourly, inserted presence of kinship on edgy borderlands

To the extent that comfortable people in lavish parlours look out on struggling children in muddy lanes, kinship is insulted. In our world of 'us' and 'them', 'rich' and 'poor', the idea of brothering or sistering is limping. With the exception of ministering in initial formation, my whole active life has been committed to borderlands. I was called to be in Monaghan for the horrible years of the bombings, for fourteen years I was gifted by the deaf community in Cabra with a rich experience of inculturation, and for the past thirty-three years I have lived a life of mutual gift-exchange as an inserted neighbour in areas of socio-economic struggle: North Wall, North Strand and Cherry Orchard. Trying to do 'what is loving' when positioned with people who are struggling with deafness or with poverty is my call to presence. Hand in glove with this venture has been the challenge to open my own soul to risk, allowing the beauty, truth, goodness and love of pained humanity to transform my heart. There has been a persistent, stirring, awkward, ultimate dynamic, which moves me to wonder and to action. This deep, gentle stirring is the diamond of God's laser light directing my journey.

Pottering around North Wall where I work, or around Cherry Orchard where I live, I am constantly asked the same unsettling questions, in various terms and by different pained faces: Is love alive? How can we stand strong as a family or as a community when the disruptive sands are constantly shifting beneath our feet to favour the well off? Where is hope? My fragile faith helps me at times to respectfully listen to these and other awkward questions and not to take short cuts in attempting an answer. The story of Jesus also helps me not to run away but to remain anchored in kinship with pained, beautiful, desperate people, and maybe together we are better able to hear the seed of mystery growing. Sometimes, I do close off and look in a different direction. At other times, I just cannot escape the wonder.

I know that I regularly get a pulse of prolonged epiphany at the Five Lamps when I am overwhelmed with the realisation that I enjoy the people of the inner-city and that they hold me as a brother. In sharing stories of miscarriages, drug addictions and heartbreak and in relishing celebrations, sing-songs and small victories, there is a vibrant, unquenchable soul-force of down-to-earth love. A mutual gift-exchange of friendship and of self-giving is on offer.[3]

2. Advocacy – empowering voiceless people to speak truth to power

Over the years in the North Wall community, I've participated in direct action, in oral hearings and in conversations with banks' ethics committees in the IFSC in order to better the lives of local people. Penning this reflection, I'm still a bit stiff from a 500 km, six-day cycle from the Poverty Stone in Dublin to the Poverty Stone in Paris promoting Agenda 2030 and its seventeen Sustainable Development Goals. I am a former board member of ATD Fourth World Ireland and am a member of the Irish 17 October Committee, which annually marks the United Nations' International Day for the Eradication of Poverty by listening to the pained voices of the silenced.

The real experts in poverty are poor people themselves. Political, media and Church commentators have a lot to say, but the cries of the poor are ignored and silenced. Knowing people as friends, real people on the margins, I am left angry and impelled at times to take action or adopt a political stance. I just can't look away anymore or be absorbed in my own security and comfort. Continual engagement with friends stretches and exposes my heart. It keeps me seeing a bigger picture and, despite my resistance, it impels me into remaining responsible for the pain of my brothers and sisters. Those who live in acute poverty feel the additional pressure to keep their shamed 'broken wings' silent and invisible. The global goals, the 17 October commemoration and the research published by ATD Fourth World remind us to keep our eyes open to the awful reality of poverty all around us. Struggling people stand up and tell their stories of courage, of friendship and of pain, and in that moment the world is stopped and changed. People who groan journey together to a place of justice called community. These varied global pulses of energy encourage those who struggle to speak with pride and inspire those who listen to contribute to change.

3. Collaborating with the North Wall community to produce a corpus of theology in an urban, contextual genre

In 1998 the Sheriff Street flats were demolished. These flats had been home over generations to the people of the parish. In good times and in bad, the flats made the North Wall community. A platform and public forum has been set up by the local community for theological conversations, which counterbalances a lopsided definition of theology that focuses solely on ecclesial and academic concerns. Neglecting the voices of the street will not help in the construction of 'a poor Church of the poor'. To mark the ending of the flats, a small committee decided to publish a book of stories. In the years since, the community has participated in workshops conducted by Don Bisson and Jack Mostyn and to date some twenty-three books have been published. The resulting theology is freshly baked Northside coddle, slow-boiled with local, organic ingredients. When we tell our stories together, we remind each other of who we are, where we came from and how we should behave. When reading or hearing our North Wall stories, we often remember something forgotten and this allows a newness to enter our lives. In sharing our stories with people who are poor, we are changed and graced.

For the planners, the politicians, the financiers and the developers, the small enclave of the North Wall community is a significant inconvenience. The local community needs social housing, schools, adequate policing and other supportive infrastructure while those in power desire the lands by the Liffey for other purposes. Subtle and unspoken planned decline or neglect is happening on the ground. Can I invite you to take a helicopter trip above the North Wall parish, beginning with the IFSC, travelling over the neighbourhoods of Seville Place and Sheriff Street down to the Point Depot? What do you see? What are the forces and values that have driven the changes in this community over the past thirty years? Have the memories, traditions and stories of the people of the North Wall made any difference? Is social capital always the slave-child to economic capital?[4]

Tossing around our stories together can help us intuit mystery present with us in our ordinary experiences. Our stories nudge, resonate and stimulate us into connecting with the 'unseen' in our lives. Rooted in the everyday experiences of the North Wall, our human imagination responds to local stories and we begin to understand better our own lives. When

Jesus wanted to describe God's kingdom, he told an everyday story. God can never have enough of our stories. Our stories lead us to the edge of mystery, of courage, of humanity and of beauty.

4. An active contemplative spirituality of the street
I've been gifted with a Ballybough upbringing, religious formation training and masters' degrees in Christian spirituality, theology and community education. So, leading inner-city groups in Annotation 19, facilitating retreats in nine schools annually, acting as an advisory board member of the Centre for Faith and Dialogue in Glasnevin, presenting annually with community confreres, the 'Searching for the Spirit in Marginal Communities' retreat and contributing to the 'Scribbles from the Margins' newsletter are elements of our search together for an appropriate active, contemplative spirituality at the edges. Facilitating creative writing classes with the parents' group in the Life Centre is also an important way of doing soul-searching. Signals of transcendence are plentiful in the ghettos of this world, as God generously empties himself into the darkness and the joys of the struggling. God who is nailed to many crosses is to be found in the sighs, the silence, the tears and the laughter of the hurting. Jesus directed our gaze in order to help us find our incognito, masked God, primarily in the outcasts and the misfits. In our Western world, which denies such surprising incarnate presence and finds its meaning and happiness in wealth, it is important for a brother or sister to be an active, contemplative eye-opener. Equally, when living with people in extreme poverty who experience shame, pain and self-hatred, it is vital to be a conduit towards confidence, hope and love. The Edmund Rice charism is a love-story for people with broken wings, those rejected by mainstream

society. When injustice and the violence of poverty become normal and enshrined in law, then liberation, brothering and sistering and resistance become our duty. Peace and justice will be served when those who are unaffected are as outraged as those who are struggling. The opposite of poverty isn't wealth, it's justice and dignity. The evils of poverty continue to triumph as long as good people stay comfortable and look away. Edmund Rice opened his eyes and his heart to Christ present in those oppressed by poverty and injustice. Brothering and sistering is about building bridges to enjoy poor people as dance partners. Wherever men and women are condemned to live in poverty, human rights are violated and Christ is nailed again to the cross.

5. Education – the most important weapon to change our world

For the past twenty-five years, I've taught a course in personal and social education in six different inner-city educational agencies. Today I teach creative writing to a parents' group in the Life Centre along with also teaching the students there. I acted as a President's Award leader to one hundred Docklands young people and continue to be member of the St Laurence O'Toole parish folk group. Week in and week out I encounter many young adults in inner-city educational agencies. Some spirited people come to education having experienced at first hand the raw violence of poverty along with the disgraceful curse and the amazing blessing of an inner-city upbringing. Some come to school from homes where food may be in short supply, while others are eighteen years old and unable to read. In short, these young people were born on the wrong side of the track, and around here survival is often a grace. In many, many ways I am not the teacher. Daily I am being mentored. Poverty kills educational dreams and cages the dreamers. All of the students I teach are not high academic achievers. Most struggle with schooling and some have grown into unhealthy lifestyles, leading to risky behaviours that threaten their future and the futures of those around them. For one class period a week, we work on such issues as reflective living, owning our story, self-esteem, social responsibility and growth through relationships. These classes are not a magic-bullet intervention in the tough lives of these young adults, but I believe they make a difference. Hopefully, my steadfast presence, my professional care and my commitment with these students signals that I am attentive to each of them and to their stories. It witnesses to the reality that brothers and sisters are the people whose lives guarantee that the struggling will be first to benefit from my teaching, and that I will be keeping a radical eye and a kind heart open, in an effort to leave no one behind.

Conclusion: Being schooled on the street in the craft of brothering and sistering

The real window into the gospel today is in kinship with those hurting on the streets. However, I am penning this conclusion sitting in Edmund Rice's bedroom in North Richmond Street. What strikes me is that when it comes to brothering and sistering, it is not what we do that matters most, rather it is the why and the how of what we do that is important. In this reflection, I've mentioned five aspects of brothering and sistering, but, irrespective of expressions, the essential toolbox requires humility, collaboration, listening, steadfast care, openness to being changed, a contemplative eye, vulnerability and on-going learning. Being contemplative and active at the edges, we will be greatly assisted by people who are poor to re-examine and re-interpret life. Only when engaging mutually and respectfully in human webs of tenderness and transformation, will we be able to hear the song of Jesus and be the yeast of the new. In friendships with people who are poor, we are formed into becoming a Church of the poor. Like Edmund, St Francis and Martin Luther King Jr, may we look out the window and respectfully engage and be transformed alongside the hurting, ignored and forgotten.[5]

Reflection
- *Martin Byrne meets God every day in the people of the margins of the North Wall, Cherry Orchard and every other place where God has placed him. For Martin, God is not to be found in a tabernacle unless he is also found in every person you meet – and especially the vulnerable, the poor and the abandoned. And Martin insists that it is the people in the margins who bless us and transform our lives.*
- *Do we look at everyone we meet as a brother and sister?*
- *Do we see a person begging on the street or who is homeless as a person to be pitied, an object to be shunned and avoided, or do we see them as the very presence of God and a gift to us? Have we the courage to allow our hearts to be touched and changed?*

Endnotes

1 Today in Ireland, many in society, Church and religious life are looking inwards with institutional concerns prioritised. Numerous people are standing with their back to the window, with the curtains closed and the shutters sealed tight. Skilled artists of connection and kinship that inspire me are Edmund Rice, Jesus, St Francis, Gandhi, Joseph Wresinski, Gregory Boyle and Martin Luther King Jr, and the people of the North Wall continually redefine my brothering, while Pope Francis directs me to look outwards.

2 Pope Francis, Homily at Chrism Mass, 28 March 2013. Available at https://www.vatican.va/content/francesco/en/homilies/2013/documents/papa-francesco_20130328_messa-crismale.html; accessed 11 July 2022.

3 As interdependent brothers and sisters at the edges, we are fashioned from some stellar dust to which we will return.

4 Many in society, Church and religious life view poor people as dependent and deficient, awaiting to be saved by the charity and pity of the comfortable middle-class gaze. This default position of the entitled in plush parlours is offensive and wounding. Poverty is defined by the powerful into a single story of deprivation and disadvantage.

5 In uniting with the sighs of hurting humanity and of creation, I try to maintain the eyes of a brothering consciousness, though I fail mostly. Thankfully, positioned at the edges, I am regularly mentored, jolted and ravished into remembering unconditional oneness by people who struggle. That is enough.

FAITH AND A BETTER WORLD: EMBRACING THE MISSION TO SHAPE THE WORLD OF TOMORROW

Michel Camdessus

Where is the world going?
I will invite the reader to consider the problems all of us share as Christians in Europe, that is, how best to embrace our mission to shape the world of tomorrow? It is quite a vital challenge. It invites us to explore where the world is going during the next decades. It also demands that we discern how we can play our full role as Christians among those from so many different horizons, sharing the same objective, to make the world a better place for the human person.

Well, our first shared response might be to say that we have no idea. Over the past few decades, the rise of secularism, individualism, materialism and consumerism has created a new and unimagined and unimaginable world in which all hitherto accepted certainties and moral compasses have been replaced by relativism and seemingly unstoppable change and uncertainty. International relations and politics are in a state of flux. So too is the world of economics and society in general in the wake of the Covid-19 pandemic. And all of this comes in the backdrop of an environmental crisis. Little wonder we have no idea. Yet there is nothing new about this confusion and challenge facing humanity today. The writer and philosopher Albert Camus spoke of a prevailing attitude of disillusion and fatalism more than sixty years ago:

> Every generation sees itself doomed to remake the world. Mine knows that we will not do it again. But our task may be greater. It consists in preventing the world from breaking down.[1]

In these conditions, can we dare to speak about longer-term perspectives (twenty to thirty years) to better prepare for the world of tomorrow? By a kind of a paradox, the answer is yes.

'Megatrends' that point pathways to a better future
While working with a group of twenty-five high-level researchers from a variety of fields, I have spent some time over the past three years studying what awaits us around the year 2050. These researchers are not 'horoscope dealers' or 'collapsologists' (a pseudoscience which is currently in vogue). We simply tried to identify 'megatrends' – those most powerful developments which are already, more or less, silently at work in our world today. These megatrends are defined by their development, their interactions and sometimes by the conflicts between them, and will be the essential features of the years 2040–50. The fascinating thing is that history, even as we are evolving within that framework, is not yet written. In embracing the mission to shape the world of tomorrow, we are far from powerless. We are still in a position to work towards reducing the risks arising from these megatrends and to take advantage of the opportunities they offer for the common good and the possibility of a better world. These include:

1. **Demographical change:** This trend dominates all others. The global demographic progression that will see Africa, the continent of youth, confronting the rest of the world, which is an ageing world. The African population will double in the next thirty years to reach 2.5 billion by 2050. It will quadruple by 2100, reaching 4.4 billion, while Europe will have seen, in the meantime, its population decline to 650 million inhabitants. Elsewhere, the population will stagnate and regress almost everywhere. The heart of the problems of tomorrow is this: will we have a rancorous and, at times, violent confrontation or a mutually enriching relationship between Africa and Europe, just sixteen miles from its shores? This is possibly the most critical issue facing Europe.

2. **Economic growth:** Continued growth of the world economy at a rate of 3 to 3.5 per cent per year, of which 2 per cent is in Europe, 4 per cent in emerging countries and perhaps 4.5 to 5 per cent in Africa depending on the quality of external support. There are serious threats to this positive global perspective including political and economic conflicts, financial instability and the continuous widening of inequalities, all of which is are major threats to growth and to political and social equilibrium in the world.

3. **Progress in international trade:** This continues despite the current protectionist strategy and conflicts.

4. **More integrated global finances:** It should be noted, however, that this is dangerously unstable, as all the lessons of the last crisis have not been learned or else have been forgotten.

5. **An economic shift from the West to the East:** It is undeniable that we are currently experiencing a tectonic shift in economic power from the west to the east due

to a major breakthrough of emerging economies. We are witnessing an extraordinary reversal of world power relations. The G7 no longer has the legitimacy to claim to lead the world. It will represent, in 2050, only 20 per cent of world GDP as against 52 per cent in the 1980s. This shift particularly affects Europe. Europe risks being dislodged from the world's governance structures unless its countries really unite. If united, Europe would still have a major role to play in a fragmented world; it will have to choose between the union and the prospect of insignificance or being a vassal.

6. **The explosion of the middle classes in developing economies:** It is estimated that four billion more people will join the ranks of the middle classes as defined by the United Nations. Eighty-four per cent of the world's population will henceforth belong to the middle and upper classes; but this happy phenomenon will coincide with another significant emerging fact: the finiteness of natural resources.

7. **The finiteness of natural resources:** Water, energy, minerals, arable land, etc., are today being exhausted. This inescapable fact calls for a radical change. What will happen if these four billion additional members of the emerging middle classes adopt Western lifestyles, the defects and negative impact of which we are now beginning to recognise and admit?

8. **Rapid urbanisation:** In a few decades 65 per cent of human beings will live in cities, including 800 million in Africa. This will require massive investments in infrastructures for these cities so that they become centres of human civilisation and not major centres of violence and despair.

9. **The impact of climate change:** A recent report published by the Intergovernmental Panel on Climate Change

is alarming. We are far from the two degrees Celsius increase trend that was seen as acceptable by COP21.
10. **Advances in science and technology:** Breakthroughs – be they in digital, interconnectivity and access to information for all, robotics, artificial intelligence, advances in medicine, etc. – all open fascinating perspectives. But this technological and scientific revolution also presents several challenges including a massive obligation of continuous ongoing training and formation. This will be required several times in the course of life in order to address, for example, risks such as the dangers of military uses of technological breakthrough and the delusions of 'transhumanism'.
11. **New faces and forms of violence:** Terrorism and civil wars are far from being overcome in many parts of the world and are, in many regions, expanding and increasing.

This is the picture of the world that awaits us. Never in such a short time has humanity experienced changes of such magnitude. What kind of a world could emerge from these megatrends?

Reading the signs of the times and seeing blessings in disguise

Look at the world and you will see that the answers to these challenges vary. People's outlooks and reflections in emerging countries appear rather optimistic. On the other hand, in our apparently more established and developed countries – and especially in Europe – the outlook tends to be focused on the risks and challenges. Is this view correct? Possibly, but there is something demobilising, even toxic, in this doubt about our ability to move the world forward. In the global picture, could there be some features that allow for more encouraging

conclusions? Invited by Christ to seek to read the 'signs of the time', we might stop to consider some of them:
- The obligation for the world to substitute a model based on more frugality for the current model of overconsumption that is leading us to the abyss.
- The cultural and economic advantages and enrichment we owe to the tremendous possibilities of exchange, travel and meetings between peoples. We might also consider the hugely positive contribution that migrants make where they are welcomed.
- The dynamics of cooperation that civil society – especially young people – set in train at ground level both in so-called developed countries and in developing countries with a vision of a more fraternal world.
- The effort, finally, of the major religions to develop interreligious dialogue and the wonderful promises of fraternity and working together that can be seen (for example) in the joint declaration of Al Azhar Grand Imam Ahmed el-Tayyib and Pope Francis during their meeting in Abu Dhabi on 4 February 2019.

These are some of the assets that are in the hands of all of humanity today. They are not spectacular, but they are 'blessings in disguise'. All these positive elements that scepticism refuses to take account of are also part of the radical novelty of our times. They open it to hope, rejecting the disillusion that many have adopted. They invite us to action. They call us to grow. This is a great challenge, yet as prospects for a better world remain open, we must try to identify the paths that could lead to it.[2] Our group of experts has suggested five 'paths of humanity' towards a universal common good:
- Eradicate extreme poverty and reduce inequalities.

- Restore finances to their role of serving the economy.
- Change global governance to build a multipolar system for a new world.
- Respond with new wisdom to the finiteness of the planet's resources.
- Enable our cultures to face up to these challenges by mobilising all the spiritual forces of the world.

These five paths suggest nothing less than a renewal of a civilisation which is threatened everywhere. They promise the advent of a world more worthy of mankind. It is vital, therefore, to explore these pathways in a little more detail.

1. Eradicate extreme poverty and reverse the rise in inequality

These are two major Sustainable Development Goals (SDGs) of the United Nations. With the goal of eradicating extreme poverty, we are, as Europeans, in the first line facing the developing world's problems. We must, therefore, in a renewed partnership with these countries, agree to invest in all key areas of their development, including education, promoting rural jobs and supporting large urban infrastructures. The need for a new attitude towards migration obeys the same logic. The challenge is difficult and heavily loaded politically, but let us remember that nobody migrates cheerfully and that the real long-term solution is to mobilise all the necessary resources to offer training and jobs in the developing world, and especially to the young who are the future of these countries and continents. If we are serious about dealing with these two massive challenges, then we must go beyond the market for a solution and embrace budgetary donations (or what is technically called 'concessional financing'), which would provide and encourage investments in priority development projects such as education, electrification, water provision and sanitation and climate change.

Perhaps one of the most pressing issues in this regard is that of economic inequality and how we might bring about a reversal of a growing trend that has characterised global development over the past three decades. It is an undeniable and unacceptable reality that for the past thirty years, the top one per cent of world income earners have captured 27 per cent of total growth of income – as much as the bottom 70 per cent of the population. A strong probability is that this situation will continue or even increase. If we do not succeed in addressing this, we may fear that all other United Nations development goals will collapse since they all depend on a sustained rate of inclusive growth. If the present rates of inequality continue unabated, then global economic growth will slow and social cohesion and democracy (where it exists) will be undermined.

2. Put finance back into the service of the economy

Continuously, in recent decades, private finance has become more important than public finance, but frequently it has also become more predatory. This is far from the core of its business, namely the service of the economy. Bringing the banks back to the service of the economy, as at their origin, would imply the following:

- An ethical renewal learning from the collapse of the 2007-8 financial system.
- A resumption or accentuation of work in the field of standards and regulations.
- An awakening of savers to a more acute sense of their responsibilities in the investment of their savings.
- The recreation by governments of a global monetary and financial system that guarantees global stability and support.

3. A new governance for a multipolar world

The most serious threats to us – be they pollution, pandemics, climate risks, new forms of violence, etc. – are all without borders. They affect the world as a whole and can only be effectively contained if our responses are part of global strategies. Alas, the global system is now being called into question. A multipolar organisation is now essential for the world community to share a common vision and to implement a 'universal common good' that cares for the needs of all countries and peoples justly and fairly. This must be for us a key priority, together with our concern to build up in our communities, regions and countries more just and caring societies.

4. Promote the radical change in consumption patterns called for to preserve the planet

This pathway needs little elaboration, explanation or justification. It is one that is at the very forefront of an extraordinary international public opinion campaign and about which, in his powerful encyclical *Laudato Si'*, Pope Francis has admirably defined the way to address jointly the social and ecological aspects of. At the heart of this encyclical is a clear recognition between harm to the environment and harm to the poor. The cry of the earth is indeed the cry of the poor.[3]

5. Change our culture

This is the 'missing link' of a sustainable development strategy. To provide for this, a first condition is necessary. We must recognise that the culture of yesterday still holds us in its claws, as Franz Kafka said. It leads all human realities to a world of desperation, division, fear or even hatred – the radical opposite of the culture that our future calls for and

needs. Consider just two of the perverse features of the old culture:
- The dominant motivation of 'gain more to consume more and more', with greed appearing surreptitiously politically correct and settling everywhere in the heart of the collective life, causes the extravagant increase of the highest remunerations and disparities and creates unacceptable income gaps. It is endless and, ultimately, self-destructive for the individual, the community and the environment.
- The narrowness of our vision of the common good still circumscribes to the limits of our towns and villages or the borders of our countries. It is quite clear, however, that a world moving towards unity can only find the harmony it aspires to in a widely diversified culture, drawing on all its universal sources.

Imagining and recreating a new world based on love and hope ... and the gospel

It is clear that we will not go far on the first four pathways if our cultures do not adapt to the new universal horizons of a unifying world. From the earliest years in school, the rising generations should be invited to discover these new horizons, marvel at them and at the same time discover the universal dimension of their civic responsibility. They will then be better prepared to engage in the major projects of the universal common good, finding in human kinship their own fulfilment. This is the path of re-enchantment of the world. This is a task that can be exciting to and animated by all those – teachers, media managers, and politicians – who can bring to public attention the universal sense of responsibility and the new art of living called for by the world of the future. They should be joined in this effort by the wisdoms, spiritualties and religions of the world that have often been, throughout history, at the origin of the great cultures of the world. They all offer us a subversive message to counter our torpor and our defeatism. They offer a message of human solidarity and kinship. They can bring to the world, with their messages of respect for human dignity, fraternity, solidarity and peace, a decisive foundation for our commitment to a more humane world. In them – and others – we will meet men and women who are bravely fighting for a better world, often without great discourse but simply moved by the force of love and hope.

In this concert of wisdoms, spiritualities of all kinds and religions, there remains one fundamental question: will the gospel be listened to? Even Christ himself had his doubts about this. Our secularised world does not care apparently. Our Church seems discredited and its traditional language inaudible. Many of us could say, as Peter said: 'We have worked all night long but have caught nothing' (Lk 5:5). This is precisely the moment when Pope Francis invites us, as he did on the centenary of *Maximum Illud*, to renew the missionary commitment of the Church:

> I am a mission, always; you are a mission, always; every baptised man and woman is a mission. People in love never stand still: they are drawn out of themselves; they are attracted and attract others in turn; they give themselves to others and build relationships that are life-giving. As far as God's love is concerned, no one is useless or insignificant. Each of us is a mission to the world, for each of us is the fruit of God's love.[4]

But how can we act in response to this call to mission? What language can we use to reach human hearts?

Perhaps we might contemplate the examples of persons who are both attracted and attracting. They are people who love this world and its beauty, who are happy to work with others, admiring of their efforts and achievements, and who are attentive to and celebrating of the 'blessings in disguise'. They see it as their mission to unveil them and so restore hope in the world; above all, sharing the joy and gratitude to be welcoming in community and working for the common good, wherever they find themselves. Very naturally then, the conditions of a genuine dialogue will develop for them. But what words do they use to share what burns in their hearts?

Cardinal Roger Etchegaray – a dear and admired friend of mine who passed away in 2019 – expressed his long and beautiful experience of such dialogues thus:

> These dialogues are a joyful part of our mission, but they are not a kind of picnic, each of the friends dumping his basket on the blanket. What these dialogues require is an armful of humility, a little bit of boldness, a pinch of tact, a heart of the poor rather than of the wealthy, adopting the attitude of somebody asking for hospitality instead of offering.[5]

In other words: asking this agnostic world to give hospitality for our faith, instead of lecturing it about religion and ethical prescriptions.

The cardinal added, of course, that mission must always go together with prayer and the sharing of the Word of God and of the Eucharist. It also requires a permanent attention to the problems and keeping hope for our society in the light of Christian social teaching while we allow our hearts to be broadened to the universal horizon of a world in its progress towards unity. If we listen to wise words of Cardinal

Etchegaray, consider the five 'paths of humanity' and reflect on the wonderful and inspirational examples of those whom the reader will have encountered in this book, then we may indeed embrace the mission and shape a better world of tomorrow in which faith and reality chime.

Reflection
- *Through his teachings and actions, Jesus invites us to consider another way of living – another way of being. He invites us to imagine anew and dare to create a world based on love of the other and love of God – a world in which selfishness, greed and power are replaced by humility, service and compassion. Michel Camdessus demonstrates that such a world is indeed possible and that if we are prepared to open our eyes and read 'the signs of the times' – and courageous enough to act accordingly – then a hope for a new horizon for humanity beckons. This is the difficult and dangerous path of discipleship – of the missionary who sees the possible in the seemingly impossible, the 'yet-to-be-realised' future in the apparent darkness and pessimism that persists in the present today. And it is a road that has been undertaken and embraced by the contributors to this book with joy and boundless energy.*
- *Do we have the wisdom and understanding to discern the 'paths of humanity' laid down by Michel Camdessus or do we – like so many others – look on the world with closed eyes?*
- *Do we have the courage to bring our vision of a new world to the public discourse and seek to change minds and hearts by an example of Christian witness?*
- *Dare we reach out to others in fraternity and solidarity and seek to walk together as brothers and sisters in love and hope to bring about a new redeemed world?*

Endnotes

1. Albert Camus, in his acceptance speech upon being awarded the Nobel Prize for Literature (10 December 1957).

2. On this, see also Nicholas Stern, *The Best of Centuries or the Worst of Centuries: Leadership, Governance and Cohesion in an Interdependent World – Fulbright Legacy Lecture,* London: Grantham Research Institute on Climate Change and the Environment and Centre for Climate Change Economics and Policy, London School of Economics and Political Science, 2018. Available at www.lse.ac.uk/GranthamInstitute/wp-content/uploads/2018/06/Stern_The-best-of-centuries-or-the-worst-of-centuries.pdf; accessed 11 July 2022.

3. See, for example, *Laudato Si'*, 25.

4. Pope Francis, *Baptized and Sent: The Church of Christ on Mission in the World* (Message for World Mission Day 2019), Vatican: Libreria Editrice Vaticana, 9 June 2019.

5. Cardinal Roger Etchegaray was a much loved and respected figure in the Curia and served as president of the Pontifical Council for Justice and Peace and president of the pontifical council *Cor Unum*. A close advisor to Pope John Paul II, he played a leading role in numerous areas including interfaith dialogue and the promotion of peace and human rights.

Postscript
LOOKING OUT THE WINDOW ONTO THE WORLD AND RESPONDING AS GOD ASKS

Angela Miyanda

> To say that I am made in the image of God is to say that love is the reason for my existence, for God is love. Love is my true identity. Selflessness is my true self. Love is my true character. Love is my name.[1]

We are born for a reason. We are born to fulfil a purpose, the all-purpose of our being, the very reason why God placed us on this earth. One day, we will stand before God to testify whether we achieved what was intended for us. What answer will we give? Will we say that we lived our lives without living for the purpose which God has intended? Will we not even consider that we had a purpose at all? How do we identify our purpose in life, the very reason why we were created?

It seems that many people in the world today do not see the purpose that God lays before them. Some spend all their time fruitlessly seeking a purpose for life but never understanding what that purpose is. In a world in which selfishness and greed are seen as guiding principles, it is little wonder that some people follow these 'false purposes' and live purely for themselves. Some have abandoned God altogether and close their eyes and ears to what he calls them to do. Yet the word of God is clear: 'For mortals, their days are like grass; they flourish like a flower of the field' (Ps 103:15). So, we are called to bloom and to shine God's love on our fellow brothers and sisters – to live out the reason for our being and our living.

God shows us the way
God does not speak in riddles nor does he hide himself from us. What he calls us to do, to be, to become are very clear. In the passage from Matthew 25 – 'The Judgement of the Nations' – Jesus calls on his disciples to feed the hungry, give drink to the thirsty, dress the naked, care for those in need and welcome the stranger. This is not an optional 'extra'; rather it is something we *must* do, for it is through the poor, the marginalised and those in need that we do God's will and encounter God himself. Jesus makes it very clear and plain: 'Just as you did it to one of the least of these who are members of my family, you did it to me' (Mt 25:40). And Jesus did not teach through words alone but through actions. Again and again in the gospels we find Jesus reaching out with compassion to those in need – and especially to the poor, the sick and the suffering, to lepers, widows and orphans who had been abandoned or excluded by society. This is what he calls on each of us to do if we are to truly achieve our godly purpose on earth – to serve those in the margins and to find God through living out the gospel message of love, compassion and service.

In my own way, I have sought to respond to the call to live out the purpose God has given to me. I have worked with vulnerable children for over twenty years in Zambia through establishing an orphanage in Lusaka that provides these young people with the love and care that God intends for them. I have been blessed to work among the poor in the villages in Zambia and have found that my life has been so fulfilled through responding to God's call to hear the cry of the poor and to act. I cannot imagine life without thinking of those in need and knowing that if we place our trust in God we can be his instruments in the world.

Answering God's call to live life to the full
In this book we have encountered men and women from all around the world who have deliberately chosen to lead their lives according to the purpose that God intended for them and to reach to help the needy where they encounter them. Like Edmund Rice, they looked out the window onto our global world, they saw and they acted. As each of us pursue our passion of helping those in need, may we find in ourselves the best gift we can share with others – God's love and compassion.

If we believe in the gospel message in Matthew 25 and accept its challenge, we can stand confidently before God to give account of what we did for our fellow men and women. God who is love and who formed us in his image and likeness calls on us to be that love in the spaces where love is absent. We are indeed his hands and his feet, his presence among his abandoned people. Let us continue to ignore the critics and sceptics and to encourage other people to live their lives for others as God asks. Then you will have lived a godly purposed life – to the glory of God the Father.

Endnote

1. Thomas Merton, *New Seeds of Contemplation,* Boulder, Colorado: Shambhala, 2003, p. 63.

Contributors

Una Agnew is a St Louis Sister and emerita professor of the Milltown Institute where she lectured in the spirituality department for over thirty years. One of her areas of research is the spirituality of the poet Patrick Kavanagh and she is the author of *The Mystical Imagination of Patrick Kavanagh: A Buttonhole in Heaven*. She also scripted and recorded, with her brother Art Agnew, a triple CD entitled *Love's Doorway to Life: An Alternative Biography of Patrick Kavanagh*, featuring more than fifty poems and excerpts from the poet's work. Doctor Agnew is a founder member of the All-Ireland Spiritual Guidance Association (AISGA).

Don Bisson is a Marist Brother of the United States Province. Don has studied the relationship between Jungian analytical psychology and spiritual direction for over forty years. On his journey as a religious, he has ministered to African Americans, Latinx and new immigrants from around the world in Oakland, California; Chicago, Illinois; and New York City. His passion at this moment is training spiritual directors for the inner city.

Martin Byrne is from Ballybough in Dublin's north inner city. He commenced his teaching as a Christian Brother in Co. Monaghan in 1971 and later spent three periods in novitiate formation ministry. For fourteen years he taught as a catechist with the community of deaf people at Cabra, Dublin, and for the past thirty-three years he has engaged in educational and other ministries in Dublin's North Wall and north inner-city. An initiator of the Edmund Rice Awards, Martin's passion for urban, contextual theology has resulted in twenty-four annual books, telling the story of God's presence in the North Wall community.

Michel Camdessus is one of the most prominent lay Catholics in the world today. An expert in economics and global development, Michel has played a key role in the Vatican's campaign for the abolition of the burden of debt in the developing world for more than twenty years. In 2000 Dr Camdessus was appointed by Pope John Paul II to serve as a lay member of the Pontifical Council for Justice and Peace and he has been a key advisor to the Vatican ever since on Catholic social teaching. In response to Pope Francis' 'Letter to the People of God' (2018), Michel Camdessus and a group of other leading lay Catholics issued a new manifesto for the Church entitled *Transformer L'Église catholique*, inviting all Catholics to consider the question 'What kind of Church would we like to see emerge from the "great trial" we are going through?' Among numerous other international organisations, Michel Camdessus is a member of the African Progress Panel.

Darryl Cronin is a descendant of the Maramanindsji people in the Daly River region of the Northern Territory and Kalkadoon people around Mt Isa in Queensland, Australia. He is the coordinator and researcher for the First Nations programme at the Edmund Rice Centre in Sydney where he researches issues of Indigenous rights and justice. Darryl has a doctorate from the University of New South Wales, a master's degree in environmental law from Macquarie University and an undergraduate bachelor's degree in law from Adelaide University. He has worked in academia and with Aboriginal organisations.

Sheila Curran is an eco-feminist theologian and a member of the Congregation of the Sisters of Mercy, Northern Province, Ireland. She holds a doctorate in practical theology, and an MA in biblical ministry from the Catholic Theological Union, Chicago, an MA in equality studies from University College Dublin and a degree in social work from the University of Ulster, Jordanstown, Belfast. Sheila worked in inner-city Dublin and in Peru for many years. Her ministry and research have been shaped by her experience of living and working with a focus on justice and equality. She is the coordinator of Mercy Global Presence in Ireland.

Jim Deeds is an author, poet and pastoral ministry worker living in the wounded and wonderful city of Belfast. His work takes him all over Ireland and beyond, giving him a sense of the mood of the country and, in particular, of the Church communities where he spends much of his working life. An avid walker, Jim enjoys the hills and mountains of his native city, often to be found with his dogs, walking, praying and developing ideas for the books, articles and chapters he writes. His walks regularly take him past the Christian Brothers school where he was educated and, as he describes it, made fit for life.

Aidan Donaldson has worked with the Edmund Rice Network for more than three decades. A former lecturer in the department of scholastic philosophy at Queen's University Belfast and at St Malachy's Junior Seminary, he taught religious education at St Mary's CBGS and also acted as school chaplain. He is a leading member of the Edmund Rice Developing World Immersion Programme and the Westcourt Social Justice Centre. Doctor Donaldson currently works as educational consultant to the Catholic Schools Support Service for the Diocese of Down and Connor and is a noted author who has published numerous books and articles on a wide range of subjects including philosophy, education and theology.

Gladys Ganiel is a sociologist at Queen's University in Belfast, Northern Ireland. She is author of many books, including the award-winning *The Deconstructed Church: Understanding Emerging Christianity* (with Gerardo Marti), *Considering Grace: Presbyterians and the Troubles* (with Jamie Yohanis), and *Unity Pilgrim: The Life of Fr Gerry Reynolds CSsR*. She has written numerous academic articles on religion, conflict and reconciliation; and religion and change in Ireland. She also is on the board of the 4 Corners Festival, an inter-church festival in Belfast that promotes Christian unity and reconciliation.

Maria Garvey has dedicated her life to revealing and bringing the gifts hidden in the margins of society to the centre. Sharing life in community with children and adults with disabilities, people with fragile mental health, men and women who are homeless and others whose lives are diminished by limiting labels bears witness to Maria's conviction that our shared vulnerability is the dwelling place of authentic connection and true belonging. A founder and former leader of L'Arche Communities in Ireland, Maria has more recently been offering training, retreats and workshops to individuals, organisations and community groups both nationally and internationally, accompanying people on their journeys through dark and challenging times, reconnecting them to themselves, to one another and to their soul's true purpose.

Denis Gleeson, a Christian Brother, has taught at all levels of education in Belfast. A former headmaster of St Mary's Christian Brothers Grammar School, Belfast, he served on numerous boards of governers, on the Council for Catholic Maintained Schools, Northern Ireland, and on the governing body of the Marino Institute of Education in Dublin. Qualified in education, theology and Christian spirituality, his interests include school ethos, religious education, pastoral care, iconography and adult spirituality. He helped establish the Westcourt Centre in Belfast and the Edmund Rice Schools Trusts in the Republic of Ireland and Northern Ireland. An author, spiritual director and retreat facilitator, he is a committed member of Contemplative Outreach.

Phil Glendenning is director of the Edmund Rice Centre for Justice and Community Education, president of the Refugee Council of Australia and co-founder and former national president of Australians for Native Title and Reconciliation (ANTaR). He has also served on the boards of the Australian Council for Social Service (ACOSS), various committees of the Australian Council for Overseas Aid and the Centre for an Ethical Society. Phil led the research team for the 'Deported To Danger' series that monitored asylum seekers in twenty-two countries, and which resulted in the documentary *A Well Founded Fear*. He holds an honorary doctorate from the Australian Catholic University; the Sir Ron Wilson Award for Human Rights; the Eureka Democracy Award; and the Order of Australia (AM) award.

Lorna Gold is director of movement building with FaithInvest. She lectures in the Department of Applied Social Studies in Maynooth University. Prior to her current roles, she led Trócaire's Policy, Research and Advocacy for almost two decades, until April 2020. She holds a PhD in Economic Geography from the University of Glasgow. Doctor Gold is acting-chair of the board of the Global Catholic Climate Movement and is a member of the recently established Vatican Commission on the post-COVID world. Her most recent book *Climate Generation – Awakening to our Children's Future* was described by Naomi Klein as 'an anguished journey into the heart of the climate crisis.' It tells her personal story of waking up to the ecological emergency as a mother, academic and activist. Her academic research interests include just transition, civil society movements and the role of faith groups in climate activism.

John McCourt, born in Dundalk, Ireland, was educated by the Christian Brothers and entered the congregation in 1962. He taught in the Abbey Primary School in Newry and in the CBS Secondary School in Belfast before being assigned to the Christian Brothers' mission in Zambia in 1976. John was to minister there, with distinction, in a variety of roles, for forty years. He served as headmaster in Livingstone; as a member of the Brothers' leadership team; as director of formation; as director of an education programme in the prison in Mongu and as college chaplain in both Mongu and Lusaka. He returned to Ireland in 2018.

Peter McVerry is a Jesuit priest and a renowned and tireless advocate for marginalised and deprived people in Ireland. While working in inner-city Dublin, Fr McVerry opened a hostel for young homeless people in 1979. The organisation,

Contributors

originally called the Arrupe Society, was subsequently renamed the Peter McVerry Trust. It now has twenty-five hostels, four drug treatment centres and five hundred and fifty apartments. He has written on many issues relating to homeless people, such as housing, drugs, juvenile justice, the gardaí, the prisons and education. A distinguished writer, his works include *The Meaning is in the Shadows*; *Jesus – Social Revolutionary?*; *The God of Mercy, the God of the Gospels* and *A Dose of Reality*. Father McVerry has received many prestigious awards for his work, including being named Irish Person of the Year in 2005, and was granted the Freedom of Dublin in 2014.

Angela Miyanda is the former deputy first lady of Zambia. She is the director of Angels in Development (AID) in Lusaka, which works with orphans and people suffering from HIV/AIDS from the townships in that region. Her most involved initiative is an orphanage in Kabwata in Lusaka which provides medical support, education and accommodation for ninety children in Lusaka, along with all that is needed to support these vulnerable children. She is also a key partner in the building of the community school, a medical centre and income-generating projects in Old Kabweza in the bush outside Lusaka. This project includes building a borehole water system, school rooms, accommodation and medical facilities for the children and local community.

Lesley O'Connor, from Dublin, lives in Tramore, County Waterford with her daughter. Her working life with the Brothers of Charity was driven by human rights concerns for people with intellectual disabilities. Lesley is motivated by interfaith dialogue and contemplative living. This led her to Contemplative Outreach, the contemplative network founded by Cistercian monk Thomas Keating. She leads retreats and currently serves on the *lectio divina* service team of Contemplative Outreach. Lesley is a coach in transformational leadership with the Mastery Foundation, empowering those engaged in ministry and reconciliation work.

Pádraig Ó Fainín was born in Waterford in 1957 and grew up (literally) in the shadow of Mount Sion in a family steeped in the tradition and ethos of Edmund Rice. He attended Mount Sion CBS, qualified as a primary school teacher and then spent thirty-six years in St Joseph's CBS in Dublin, the last fifteen years of which were as principal. In 2004 Pádraig commenced his involvement in the missions in Zambia through the Edmund Rice Developing World Immersion Programme and soon found himself at home in the Sables project in the town of Kabwe in central Zambia. This is a centre which provides food, clothing, medical care, emergency accommodation, counselling, education and vocational training for the most vulnerable young people, including orphans and street children. And, for a considerable time, it literally became his home, as Pádraig and his wife, Emer, left Dublin to spend almost five years living in the centre. They have recently returned to Ireland in order to best serve the needs of Sables through raising funds and awareness of the work of this wonderful facility.

Don O'Leary is director of the Cork Life Centre, a voluntary organisation set up by the European province of Christian Brothers to offer an alternative learning environment to young people who find themselves outside the mainstream secondary education system. Don has led this community of learning since 2006. His background is in youth and community work and he has worked and continues to work with numerous youth and community groups. He is a passionate advocate for human rights and children's rights in particular. He is an activist with a commitment to system reform and services that meet the needs of all children and young people and to working towards a society where no one is left behind.

Philip Pinto is a Christian Brother living and working in India. Much of his almost sixty years as a Christian Brother has been spent in the ministry of leadership – including two terms as congregation leader and in spiritual renewal. He is passionate about religious life and the search for God in our world today. His mother was a convert who instilled in him the conviction that God is bigger than any religion, and that every religion holds important insights into the meaning of life. He is interested in sharing his experience with other groups also keen on understanding the vision of Jesus in today's world.